FamilyFun
Boredom Busters

**Pipe-cleanosaurus,
page 28**

FamilyFun
Boredom Busters

Edited by Deanna F. Cook
and the experts at FamilyFun magazine

NEW YORK

This book is dedicated to the readers of *FamilyFun* magazine

Printed in the United States of America. For information address Disney Editions, 114 Fifth Avenue, New York, NY 10011-5690.

The activities and photographs in this book
were previously published in *FamilyFun* magazine.

FamilyFun magazine is a division of Disney Publishing Worldwide.
To order a subscription, call 800-289-4849.

FamilyFun magazine

BOOK EDITORS: Deanna F. Cook, Alexandra Kennedy, and Catherine Newman
CONTRIBUTING EDITORS: Jonathan Adolph, Dawn Chipman, Barbara Findlen, Ann Hallock,
Cindy A. Littlefield, and Katherine Whittemore
COPY EDITORS: Laura MacKay and Paula Noonan
EDITORIAL ASSISTANTS: Jean Graham, Julia Lynch, and Ellen Harter Wall
PICTURE EDITOR: Mark Mantegna
PRODUCTION EDITORS: Jennifer Mayer and Dana Stiepock
TECHNOLOGY COORDINATOR: Tom Lepper
CONTRIBUTING CRAFT DEVELOPER: Maryellen Sullivan

Impress, Inc.

CREATIVE DIRECTOR: Hans Teensma
DESIGN DIRECTOR: Carolyn Eckert
PROJECTS DIRECTOR: Lisa Newman
DESIGN ASSOCIATE: Leslie Tane
ART ASSOCIATE: Jen Darcy

The staffs of **FamilyFun** and **Impress, Inc.,**
conceived and produced *FamilyFun Boredom Busters* at
244 Main Street, Northampton, MA 01060

In collaboration with
Disney Editions, 114 Fifth Avenue, New York, NY 10011-5690

Library of Congress Cataloging-in-Publication Data on file.

First Edition
1 3 5 7 9 10 8 6 4 2

ISBN 0-7868-5361-1

Acknowledgments

FamilyFun Contributors

Special thanks to the following *FamilyFun* magazine writers for their wonderful boredom busters: Rani Arbo, James Barr, Mira Bartok, Lynne Bertrand, Rebecca Boucher, Heidi Illingworth Boyd, Barbara Bruns, Cynthia Caldwell, Marie Cecchini, Ronnie Citron-Fink, Tobye Cook, Maryellen Kennedy Duckett, Megan Fowlie, Susan Fox, Robin Granger, Ellen Haas, Suzanne Haiker, Linda Masternak Justice, Marty Kaminsky, Mollie Katzen, Amy King, Susan Lapinsky, Jean Lemlin, Brenda Lindsay, Jane Maddin, Nancy Mades, Shoshana Marchand, Colin McEnroe, Charlotte Meryman, Diana Baird N'Diaye, Kevin Nelson, Rebecca Lazear Okrent, Mary Therese Otis, Leslie Garisto Pfaff, Jodi Picoult, Barbara Poisson, John Porcino, Alicia Potter, Susan Purdy, Denise Dahlin Radecke, Barbara Rowley, Debra Judge Silber, Nanciann Smith, Sue Stauffacher, Edwina Stevenson, Sherry Timberman, Emily B. Todd, Laura Torres, Penny Warner, Natalie Walker Whitlock, and Lynn Zimmerman.

FamilyFun Readers

Special thanks also to the following *FamilyFun* readers who shared the boredom busters that have been a success with their families: Steve Argue, Kathy Bias, Jennifer Caputo, Elaine Chenette, Margaret Connor, Terri Delzer, Robin Fennelly, Carol Fitzgerald, Gail Fournier, Laura Frazier, Robin Giese, Jo Ella Graney, Barbara Graydon, Debra Griggs, Lucy Hardy, Tracy Hodapp, Shirley Hooey, Meredith Jack, Linda B. Jennings, Theresa Jung, Amy King, Maribeth Knierim, Sharon Lawton, Mary Leonhardt, Connie Lowry, Dee Martin, Melissa McComas, Pat McGough-Wujcik, Cindy McNeely, Janae McSpadden, Rachel Meyer, Susan Michalczak, Julie Miller, Lori Murray, Kim Novato, Christine Nowaczyk, Deanne Nutaitis, Susan O'Brien, Karin Overby, Chandra Peters, Candace Purdom, Julie Reimer, Carol Saunders, Peggy Schulten, Dawn Segura, Madonna Sheridan, Kirsten Son, Becky Sprague, Lori Waters, and Patricia Zeman-Murphey.

FamilyFun Staff

With gratitude to all the staff of *FamilyFun*'s art and editorial departments, who directed all of the original work, especially Cindy A. Littlefield and Ginger Barr Heafey. In addition to the book staff credited on the previous page, we'd like to acknowledge the following staff members: Douglas Bantz, Nicole Blasenak, Jodi Butler, Grace Ganssle, Moira Greto, Michael Grinley, Melanie Jolicoeur, Elaine Kehoe, Gregory Lauzon, Adrienne Stolarz, Mike Trotman, and Sandra L. Wickland.

About the Editors of *FamilyFun Boredom Busters*

Deanna F. Cook, Manager of Creative Development of *FamilyFun* magazine, is the editor of the FamilyFun book series, which includes *FamilyFun Crafts* and *FamilyFun Cookbook,* all from Disney Editions, and the author of *The Kids' Multicultural Cookbook* and *Kids' Pumpkin Projects* from Williamson. She lives in Florence, Massachusetts, with her husband, Doug, and her two active daughters, Ella and Maisie.

Alexandra Kennedy is the Editorial Director of *FamilyFun* magazine and *Disney Magazine.* She and her husband, James Haug, rarely have an opportunity to be bored, thanks to their two sons, Jack and Nicky. They all live and play in Northampton, Massachusetts.

Catherine Newman is a *FamilyFun* contributing editor. She lives in Easthampton, Massachusetts, with her family, which, thanks to the sparkling imagination and mischief of two-year-old Ben, is never bored.

Special thanks to all the photographers, stylists, and models for their excellent work, which first appeared in *FamilyFun* magazine.

This book would not have been possible without the help at Disney Editions, especially of Duryan Bhagat, Janet Castiglione, Wendy Lefkon, Jill Newman, and Jody Revenson.

Contents

Lunch Guests,
page 178

Doggy Digs,
page 75

CHAPTER ONE

Ready, Set, Play!

What do you do when there's nothing to do? Try a healthy dose

of family fun and games.

IT'S NINE A.M. on a Saturday — the kind of day that is fairly bursting with possibility. Still, the house needs cleaning, the lawn has to be mowed, and that laundry is piled high. So what are you going to do? Squander the day on chores while the kids sit around bored and complain that there's nothing to do? Or find some time to make the day special and have fun together as a family?

At *FamilyFun* magazine, we know this dilemma all too well. Our readers, our contributors, and the parents on our staff all understand that family life is a real juggling act between what we have to do and what we want to do — kick back and have fun with our kids. We may not be able to give you any extra hours to get your chores done, but we can share with you our secrets for making the most of the time you do have.

In this book, we have gathered hundreds of our favorite activities from *FamilyFun*. Each project is family tested and proven to keep boredom at bay.

Some of the ideas are as simple as playing a calculator game when you're waiting in the doctor's office (see page 23) or blowing a double bubble with soap in the backyard (page 36). Others are more involved — crafting a hiking stick for a nature walk (page 124), learning and playing a new game with the kids in the neighborhood (Chapter Three), or cooking up a silly sweet in the kitchen (pages 186 to 191).

The next time boredom strikes in your household, have your kids flip through these pages and flag a few activities to try. Once you settle on one, you will have the perfect excuse for throwing your responsibilities to the wind. What's more, the project will not require much money or planning — only a firm resolve to seize the day.

So put the rake back in the garage. Childhood doesn't last forever, and your garden, rest assured, will get by just fine until tomorrow. And remember, sometimes a single special afternoon is all you need to make the memory of a lifetime.

Jump-starting Activities

Classic Boredom Busters

- Make a paper bag puppet
- Paint a face on a rock
- Construct a cootie catcher
- Design a paper airplane
- Juggle sock balls
- Build a couch-cushion fort
- Blow bubbles
- Play slapjack
- Fly a kite
- Sing along with your favorite tunes
- Read a story together
- Start a collection (rocks, buttons, bottle caps — whatever's easy to find around the house or yard)
- Make a paper-clip chain
- Draw your favorite person (or place, cartoon character, sport, etcetera)
- Bowl with a tennis ball and a few empty plastic soda bottles
- Cut up a catalog and make a collage
- Dab watercolor designs onto paper coffee filters
- Do a jigsaw puzzle

IF YOU'VE EVER TRIED to pull your child away from an elaborate game of make-believe or a half-done drawing of outer space, then you know the problem is not *keeping* kids interested in an activity — it's getting them started. This book is both a planning tool and an emergency resource: the more involved activities can be planned for and set up in advance, while the hundreds of quick, simple activities can serve as instant antidotes to the inevitable lulls in your kids' imaginations. Here are a few basic tips for inspiring activity:

Post a list of your favorite boredom busters. Your kids can consult it when boredom strikes and add to it as they find new projects they love. Keep a pad of sticky notes handy for marking activities in this book.

Create fun zones. Set up places in the house for your kids to go to when they need something to do. Designate a project table where your kids can work on activities (puzzles, models, crafts) without having to clean up every time.

Nestle books in a comfy reading corner.

Be spontaneous. You'll see that the surprise factor goes a long way toward keeping your kids entertained. Choose an activity that is out of the ordinary, like making wildly decorated cupcakes (see page 186), building a geodesic dome out of newspaper (page 140), or mixing up a batch of washable window paints (see page 142).

Have a few tricks up your sleeve. For that endless snowstorm or week home sick, you'll want to have a handful of extraspecial activities planned. Set aside a giant box of new crayons or put together a box of supplies for a project in this book.

The Boredom Bottle

Here's the next best thing to a genie in a bottle — a handy stash of activities your kids can conjure up with a shake of the wrist.

1. Have your kids label a plastic bottle and decorate it with stickers.

2. Together with your kids, make a list of easy activities or challenges requiring little or no explanation and write the name of

each activity on a small paper square (see the list at left for ideas). When your kids aren't looking, you might also want to slip in a few unexpected treats, such as "Bake a batch of chocolate chip cookies."

3. Fold the paper squares in half and drop them into the bottle. When after-school boredom strikes, have your kids shake out an idea — the anticipation and surprise are sure to enhance the fun.

Gathering Objects of Fun

SOME DAYS, a small rubber ball or a handful of shells is all your child needs to keep busy for hours. Other times, all the board games in the world won't fill the deep pit of boredom. Our solution? Keep on hand a good supply of versatile toys and materials — many of the supplies called for in this book will inspire imaginative play. In addition to inviting creativity, a well-stocked craft closet, pantry, and tool kit save you needless trips to the store when your child has the urge to tackle a project. Here are some basics:

Craft supplies. For instant craft projects, stock up on paper (white, construction, and a large roll of newsprint), paints (tempera, watercolor, and acrylic craft), paintbrushes, scissors, glue (glue sticks, white glue, and a low-temperature glue gun), markers, crayons, colored pencils and a sharpener, tape, and clay. Keep your craft supplies stocked, well organized, and accessible in a canvas shoe bag like the one at right.

Game basics. Stock your garage with balls, sports equipment (baseball gloves and bats, soccer balls, bikes and helmets), marbles, and colored chalk. Inside, stack a low shelf with board games, puzzles, and playing cards.

Toys and activity kits. Assemble playthings in well-labeled boxes and store them in key places around your house.

Gather some office supplies, such as paper clips and memo pads, in a Junior Executive Kit (see page 23) and leave them by your desk. Keep a musical instrument box (page 90) by the stereo for impromptu jams. Stock a magnifying glass, bug jar, and butterfly net in a nature kit in the garage.

Eco-friendly materials. Don't toss handy recyclables, such as egg cartons, toilet paper tubes, bottles, and cardboard boxcs — save them for craft projects and make-believe props. Collect nature finds, such as acorns, shells, and shiny rocks for game pieces and quick crafts.

Tools. Providing a selection of kid-size tools is an inviting way to say, "Wanna help?" Have on hand a junior set of cooking utensils (cookie cutters, rolling pins, and more) and kid-size carpentry or gardening tools.

Extras. As you select projects from this book, examine the materials list closely to see what you and your child need to complete the project. Sometimes little things — like googly eyes, pipe cleaners, or craft foam — can make all the difference.

Ready, Set, Play!

Encouraging Independent Play

Surprise Bags

Fill paper bags with a few ingredients for fast fun and set them aside for emergencies (sick days, snow days, terrible moods, after-school blues). Here are some suggestions:

✦ A bunch of googly eyes, pom-poms, and glue for making creatures

✦ A recipe for play clay (see page 14) with all the ingredients to make it, plus a few sculpting tools

✦ A set of paper dolls, plus scissors and gift wrap for making a wardrobe

✦ A yo-yo and a book of yo-yo tricks

✦ A pair of plain sneakers and some fabric markers

✦ A magnifying glass, a "spy notebook," and a secret code to break

IN AN IDEAL WORLD, our kids would get home from school and we would give them our full attention — the phone would never ring, bills would never need to be paid, and the house would look after itself. But in our actual lives, there are times when our kids need to fend for themselves while we work behind the scenes to make a home for them, and we don't always want to pop in a video. This book is full of projects and ideas kids of all ages can carry out successfully on their own. We've gathered a few tips to encourage further independence:

Encourage pretend play. Left to their own devices, children are inclined to see the world as a place of endless opportunity for fantasy-filled fun. The smallest catalyst from you can inspire wonderful reactions. Gather a pile of old clothes and accessories (see page 80) and see what kinds of costumes they inspire. Or pull a bunch of chairs into a line, and before you know it, your kids will be on an imaginary train headed for the North Pole.

Create play scenarios. Challenge your kids to build a palace for their dolls or to set up a grooming station for their animals. How about a Grand Prix for toy cars? Multiuse toys like blocks, dolls, and adventure sets really foster imaginative play.

Rotate their toys. When kids' toys are out of sight (a few favorites excepted), they are also out of mind. By keeping a box of these playthings hidden away, you will always have an ace in the hole when boredom creeps up. An unexpected reunion with a forgotten Barbie, set of figurines, or board game can really spark a dull afternoon. Plus, storing some toys in a cupboard means your kids will have less stuff out to keep tidy.

Make cleanup part of the project. Not only will your kids learn responsible habits, but that final five minutes of cleanup may just give you the extra time you need to finish your own project.

Playing With a Purpose

WHEN YOUR KIDS have already put together their puzzles and built an entire city in their sandbox, the best boredom buster might be a real job. If they are young enough, they probably still think housecleaning is some kind of game, and cooking is a science experiment. By helping out, your kids will become contributing members of your household, and they'll have a whole lot of fun doing it. Just be sure to thank them enthusiastically when they finish.

Enlist their help. Fill a bucket with soapy water and let your kids scrub the car or shampoo the dog. Turn on the music and see if they can pick up all their toys by the end of the song. The more fun you make the chore, the more likely it is your kids will chip in.

Do a good deed. Ask for kids' advice about random acts of kindness: they might craft a get-well card for a friend with the flu, bake cookies for an elderly neighbor, or even clean their old toys and donate them to a child in need.

Give kids real responsibility. Kids love to be praised, and they love to feel important. Take advantage of this by giving them challenging and rewarding tasks: watering plants, caring for pets, or cooking a pancake breakfast for the whole family.

FAMILYFUN READER IDEA

The Cleanup Game

"To make housecleaning fun, I made up an activity called the Cleanup Game. Everyone in the family takes paper and a pencil and walks from room to room looking for messes. Each of us records instructions on the paper, such as 'Pick up and fold hand towels' or 'Put away Monopoly game.' These commands are put in a bag, and everyone takes turns picking them and doing the jobs. It's a riot, and it teaches kids to notice messes."

— Carol Saunders, Livingston, New Jersey

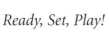

Ready, Set, Play!

Cultivating Creativity

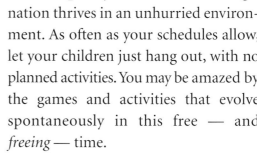

Endless Roll of Paper

What can you do with a large roll of white or butcher paper? Anything you like!

✦ Make a cheering banner to decorate the front of your house ("Welcome Home" or "Happy Spring" is reason enough to have a celebration)

✦ Draw an imaginary roadway and city for toy cars, or a magical landscape for figurines

✦ Illustrate a running story with panels you add to daily

IF NECESSITY IS the mother of invention, then boredom must be the father of creativity. We've found that sparking bored kids' imaginations requires three things: having art supplies on hand, encouraging pretend play, and creating an environment in which imaginations flourish.

Emphasize the process. When beginning a craft or cooking project, it's fine to have an end result in mind — older kids, particularly, are proud of finished projects. But try not to be so determined to follow directions that your child can't add his own flair. The end result, after all, is no more important than the steps that lead up to it.

Model enthusiasm. Your willingness to plunk a brush into a jar of paint will inspire your kids to do the same. Similarly, if you're game to join their imaginary games, your kids may feel even more excited about playing them.

Allow plenty of free time. Imagination thrives in an unhurried environment. As often as your schedules allow, let your children just hang out, with no planned activities. You may be amazed by the games and activities that evolve spontaneously in this free — and *freeing* — time.

Best-ever Play-clay Recipe

When it comes to busting boredom, a batch of this sculptable stuff is like money in the bank. Store it in airtight containers for weeks of hands-on fun.

INGREDIENTS

1 cup all-purpose flour	1 cup water
1/2 cup salt	1 teaspoon vegetable oil
1/2 teaspoon cream of tartar	Food coloring

Mix the flour, salt, cream of tartar, water, and oil in a saucepan. Cook over medium heat until it holds together (keep mixing or it will stick to the bottom of the pan). When the clay is cool enough to touch, knead it on a floured surface, divide it into smaller balls, and add a different shade of food coloring to each ball.

Making Time for Family

WE LIVE IN an overscheduled age, and there are lots of duties we parents cannot avoid. But there may be some we can postpone for the sake of creating time to spend with our families doing something fun, or doing nothing at all.

Let the chores pile up. Decide where your schedule can give a little — and let it. This may mean a shaggier lawn, it's true, but you can promise yourself to turn into the perfect homemaker after the kids leave for college. Do a project or take a field trip with them instead.

Play with your kids. Your kneeling down on the floor to *vroom* trains around with your children will give them — and you — tremendous pleasure. Throw a football around the yard. Spend the afternoon hunched over the Monopoly board. You'll feel like a kid again, and you'll get to know your own kids better.

Have a do-nothing day. Commit a full day to relaxing play with your family. This means no big outings, no big projects, and no serious enter-taining. Play the games your kids are always begging you to join in on, or sit on the floor with coloring books. Read a story together, even if your kids can read on their own. Prepare leisurely meals together.

Watch TV deliberately. Is there a show your whole family loves? By all means watch it together. There is a wealth of wonderful educational programming that can make for a fun evening tube-side. But you may want to let the television stay quiet sometimes. Keep an eye on channel surfing as an antidote to boredom.

Make Fridays Family Night. Make a weekly date to play a family game. Order a pizza (better yet, make one — see page 185). Rent a video, pop pop-corn, and snuggle under a big blanket for movie night. Eat dinner in your pajamas or all dressed up. Or have a monthly planned outing to a restaurant or show.

However you do it, making regular time for your family to spend together will guarantee a great time — and a treasure trove of wonderful memories — for all of you.

Family Traditions

Set up a monthly date with each child. Whether you go out to lunch or see a movie, both you and your child will look forward to this one-on-one time.

Keep a family journal in a prominent place in your house and encourage everybody to contribute at least one entry a week.

Talk about your day. At dinnertime, go around the table and have everyone share the Best Thing/Worst Thing that happened that day.

Have a TV-free week. Pull the plug on the TV for one week and fill your time with family activities: biking, walking, swimming.

Backpack Danglers,

page 30

CHAPTER TWO

Instant Fun

In a pinch? Kids getting bored? Thirty minutes to dinner? Try our quick games, easy crafts, and other ideas to fill 15 minutes of free time.

WHEN OUR KIDS step off the school bus after a long day of dueling fractions, they are ready to devote themselves wholeheartedly to the pursuit of fun. But by the time they unwind, eat a snack, and unload their backpacks, there's sometimes as little as a half hour of free time left before dinner.

The truth is, much of family life takes place in brief intervals: the 15 minutes you have before soccer practice; the 30 minutes until your child gets picked up for a play date; the 20 minutes riding in the car. These slices of time are usually unplanned — and unwanted. But they don't have to be. Instead of approaching them as time to kill, we advocate appreciating such snatches as time to fill.

With that carpe diem attitude in mind, we offer you a chapter full of our favorite 15-minute-and-under activities: games, crafts, and tricks to harness the bits of spare time that life offers you.

When you have a few minutes of free time, let your children pick an idea from the following pages to suit their mood and companions (or lack thereof). The projects in this chapter require only readily available supplies and very little, if any, parental assistance. Some, like The Flamingo Stance Dance on page 40, are rowdy energy burners; others, like the quick and easy Foil Family on page 24, can happily occupy a lone child when zip is in short supply. These are just a few ideas for living fully in the moments you find. To make the most of your family time, keep these fast-fun principles in mind:

Find fun where (and when) you can. Whether you're at a restaurant, in the car, or just plain waiting, you may discover that you have much more family time than you ever thought possible. Instead of making grocery shopping a chore, for instance, turn it into a field trip and send your kids on a hunt for the cheapest cornflakes or the products that match the coupons. Stuck in traffic?

Pipe Cleaner People, page 28

Peanut Pal, page 27

See who can find the most animals in passing billboards, or who can come up with the catchiest blues riff in the backseat.

Prepare an Emergency Fun Kit. Fill a bag with props and keep it on hand to chase away any sudden bouts of boredom. Consider including such versatile items as toothpicks, a rubber ball, buttons, a full deck of cards, dice, pipe cleaners, rubber bands, aluminum foil, and marbles.

Stock up on supplies. Having basic art supplies accessible can do wonders to keep your kids busy and independent. A pad of paper and a pencil, crayons and coloring books, scissors, stickers, construction paper, glue stick, and play clay — with minimal setup, these basics can spearhead a 10-minute doodle or quick paper craft.

Use your imagination. Once you get going, your kids will come up with their own quick games. When it comes to instant fun, silliness and spontaneity are true virtues.

5-minute Fun

Need some ideas for lickety-split fun? Sometimes simpler is better:

* Thumb wrestle
* Hold a jacks tournament
* Stage a silly-song session with a tape recorder
* Turn a paper tablecloth into a giant crayon canvas
* Play crazy eights
* Build structures with toothpicks and mini marshmallows
* Spin a yo-yo
* Ref an impromptu contest with an egg timer

Tabletop Games

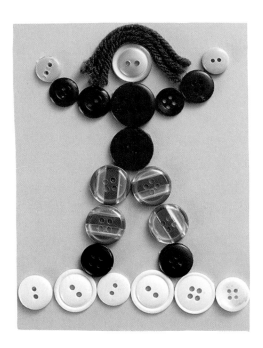

Play With Buttons

1 What do you do on those days when your kids' favorite toys suddenly lose their entertainment value? Empty out your button box on the kitchen table and try the following quick activities.

MATERIALS

Assorted buttons

Glue, fabric, yarn, poster board

Pie plate

Elastic thread

Dabble in button art: Glue buttons and bits of fabric or yarn onto poster board to create a textured portrait or landscape.

Pan for buttons: Place a pie plate on the floor near a wall, line up 10 to 12 feet away, and see who can pitch the most buttons off the wall and into the pan.

Make button jewelry: String elastic thread through the holes of assorted flat buttons, then tie it into a loop for a wrist or ankle bracelet.

Build a button tower: See who can stack the most buttons without toppling the tower.

QUICK GAME

Tabletop Hockey

2 If you want to score some instant fun on a rainy day, cut a plastic berry box in half. Invert one half and set it at one end of a table. Now your kids can line up at the opposite end and try to score by flicking button pucks into the net.

INSTANT TOY

Funny Faces

3 This felt man is a master of disguise — just give him a shake and he'll put on a new face. With a marker, draw a profile of a person, leaving out the front of his face, on a felt-covered piece of cardboard. Use a nail to poke a hole in the forehead and the neck, then loosely thread through a length of ball chain, taping the ends to the back of the cardboard. Now hold the drawing flat and jiggle it — the chain will form a nose and chin.

A Penny Pool

4 **For some quick fun on a rainy day, ask your child to guess how many drops of water he can fit on a penny. Then hand him a drinking straw for a dropper and see how close he comes to his estimate. Because water droplets cling together, he may fit as many as 24 drops if he's careful!**

Pinch Your Pennies

5 With this coin-gobbling bank, saving your pennies can become downright habit-forming.

MATERIALS

Poster board or card stock

Mason jar with a metal rim (you won't need its flat inner lid)

Glue

2 googly eyes

3 pom-poms

3 pipe cleaners

For the bug's face, cut out a poster board circle to fit inside the metal rim of the mason jar. Use scissors to cut out a rectangular mouth large enough for a quarter to drop through.

Glue on googly eyes and a pom-pom nose. Set the finished face on top of the jar opening, then screw on the rim. To add antennae, wrap a pipe cleaner around the metal rim, twisting the ends together once to secure. Then bend the ends slightly to form a V and glue pom-poms onto the tips. Use the same method to attach a pair of pincher arms to the jar just below the metal rim, this time twisting together the pipe cleaner ends to within a half inch of the tips.

FUN FACT

Here's a penny for your thoughts: the coin-y motto "E pluribus unum" means "One from many" and describes the United States (although we think it's a pretty good slogan for a family too!).

Penny Basketball

6 **Wanna shoot some hoops? Find a penny, a partner, and a tabletop and follow these NPBA (National Penny Basketball Association) instructions:**

1. Put the penny into play by spinning it on edge.

2. Trap the coin between your thumbs, one on each side of the coin.

3. With the sides of your pinkies on the table and your fingertips together (see drawing), flick the penny up with your thumbs so that it swooshes through the basket that

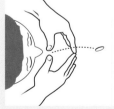

your opponent, across from you, is making with her fingers. Take turns shooting. You score two points per basket. The first player to score 10 points wins — and keeps the penny.

House of Cards

7 Requiring little more than a deck of cards and a box of toothpicks, this no-frills game is a testament to the adage that less is more.

MATERIALS

Paper and pencil

Deck of cards (including 2 jokers)

Box of toothpicks

The object of the game is to build a house (strictly two-dimensional) out of toothpicks. Whoever finishes construction first is the winner. For each player, draw a simple model house like the one below on a sheet of paper. Make sure you indicate the number of toothpicks needed (you can do this by using broken lines, one for each toothpick).

Shuffle the cards and place the entire deck facedown on the table. Players alternate picking a card from the top of the deck. Moves depend on which card you pick (see "What the Cards Mean," at right).

Once your child has chosen a card and followed the directions, she should place it facedown next to the original deck. If players run out of cards before the game ends (and it's likely that they will), reuse the discards, shuffling them first. **Tip:** Each player might vary the game by drawing a different house — a tent, say, or a treehouse.

What the Cards Mean

Any face card (king, queen, or jack): Take one toothpick and use it to build your house.

Any ace: Take two toothpicks and use them to build your house.

Joker: Put back one toothpick. (If you don't have one yet, do nothing.)

Any eight: Use one of your toothpicks to help build the house of the opponent on your right. (As with the joker, if you don't have any toothpicks yet, you don't have to do anything.)

Two of spades: Players who draw this unlucky card must put back all their toothpicks and start over.

All other cards: No value.

A Straw Stumper

8 Arrange 12 drinking straws, as shown. Can you remove two so that you're left with just two complete squares? (Answer below.)

Answer: Remove any two adjacent straws of the four inside the large square. You'll be left with a small square inside a large square.

FUN FACT

Question:

Which straw broke the camel's back?

Answer:

At .025 ounce each, that would be roughly the 786,000th!

Citrus Sipper

9 You don't need a pitcher to make this lemonade — in fact, you don't even need to stir. Simply break a peppermint stick in two and insert one half directly into an uncut lemon. Suck on the peppermint stick as you normally would, and after a few minutes (surprise!), you'll taste lemon juice! Here's how it works: as you suck on the candy, tiny holes are created, turning the stick into a straw. The sour juice of the lemon combines with the sweet and minty taste of the peppermint stick for an instant treat.

Turn Straw Into Gold

10 Just because restaurants give them out by the handful doesn't mean straws aren't a valuable raw material for the creative crafter. Consider these two nifty projects:

MATERIALS

- **Drinking straws**
- **Ping-Pong ball**
- **Tape**
- **Magazine cover**

Balancing Ball Blower

This probably demonstrates some key principle of aerodynamics, but all we know is it's cool. Carefully slice a flexible straw's end and bend out the arms. Place a Ping-Pong ball in the cradle and blow hard and steady. The ball will hover. Sheer magic!

Double-O Glider

Believe us, this thing really flies.

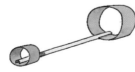

Cut two strips, 6 inches and 9 inches long and at least an inch wide, from the magazine cover. Tape into O's and slide them into slits cut in the straw's ends. Hold the straw with the small O facing forward and throw.

Home Office Kit

11 When you are busy paying bills or working at home, hand your kids this Junior Executive Kit so they can play independently. With the right supplies, business will boom.

MATERIALS

Inexpensive briefcase or plastic case

Calculator

Notebook

Pens, paper clips, and other office
   supplies

Assemble a home office kit in an old briefcase or plastic container, using assorted office supplies from your own stash. Include Post-its, a roll of tape, a stapler, paper clips, and other supplies for your pint-size CEO. For fun, include a set of business cards (printed up at a copy shop or on your home computer).

Word Processing

12 This game is great for entertaining your kids during those endless doctor's office waits. Just turn on a pocket calculator and challenge them to see how many number combinations they can come up with that spell words when the calculator is turned upside down. Here are a few numbers to get you started (for answers, see page 219).

a. 663   d. 77345   g. 7714   j. 637

b. 604   e. 5508   h. 618   k. 35007

c. 771   f. 733   i. 3045   l. 7738

Clipboards, Inc.

13 Hand your kids clipboards (to set an industrious mood) and give them each an assignment. For example, they might need to draw a treasure map, invent a better flyswatter, create a secret code, or write a mock newspaper article about what's happening outside the window.

Bored Book

One mom's list of things to do when there's nothing to do

"When my daughter, Jade, couldn't find anything to do, I came up with the perfect solution. I made a list of all the activities we have around the house, including toys, sports equipment, puzzles, and board, electronic, and computer games. I compiled the list, added pictures to make it look like a fun vacation brochure, and placed it in a three-ring binder. Because many of the toys and games were tucked away, we had forgotten what we had. Now whenever Jade and her younger sister, Jazlyn, are looking for something to do, I refer them to our book."

— Cindy McNeely, Tallahassee, Florida

Quick Crafts

Pet Rocks

14 Part of the fun with this 1970s-inspired craft is hunting for the perfect rocks to decorate. This makes it a fitting project to do after a nature hike. Encourage your kids to look for natural features in the rocks that resemble noses, chins, ears, and so on. Help little kids stick pebbles, googly eyes, and pompoms in place with double-sided tape or glue. Kids can use fun fur for hair, mustaches, and beards or apply additional features with acrylic paint.

Party of One

"To help my five-year-old, Amy, learn to entertain herself, we invented the 15-minute game. I fill paper bags with materials for a short project, seal them, and keep them for special times. For example, in one bag, I placed the makings for a bird's nest, including yarn, twigs, clay, and even candy eggs. I have also filled bags with postcards, pens, and stamps for writing to Grammy, or simply enclosed a long-forgotten toy. The game has been a hit — I get 15 minutes when I need it, and she gets a new activity to enjoy."

— Jennifer Caputo,
Lawrenceville, Georgia

The Foil Family

15 Unlike your average tin men, these foil characters have plenty of heart. All it takes is a pinch here and there to make them strike any pose your child likes.

MATERIALS

Rectangular sheet of aluminum foil (about 10 by 15 inches)

Scissors

Make two cuts down from the top of the sheet and one cut up from the bottom, as shown below (for a pet, make two cuts up from the bottom). Now scrunch together the center of the sheet to form a torso and pinch and mold the upper corners into arms and the lower corners into legs and feet. Finally, shape the upper midsection into a head and neck (the lower midsection makes the pet's tail).

Release a Paper Dove

Here's one critter that you won't mind invading your next picnic: a high-flying dove made from paper plates and plastic spoons.

MATERIALS

Paper plate
Pebble
2 plastic spoons
Rubber band
Tape
Markers

Cut the plate in half, then cut one half into three equal wedges and tape one wedge to the bottom of the intact half, as shown.

Now sandwich the pebble between the spoon bowls and bind the spoons with the rubber band.

Finally, tape the spoons to the bottom of the paper plate half and draw a face on the top spoon.

To make the dove fly, throw it like a paper airplane. Adjust the pebble size to improve flight.

Paint to Music

17 **For a quick and soulful project, let your kids put on some tunes, grab a paintbrush, and paint what they hear. Does the mood of the music suggest a color? How about painting the shape of a slow melody or moving the brush along with the energy of the rhythm? Try Vivaldi's *Four Seasons*, the Beatles, melodic pop songs with varied textures, Prokofiev's *Peter and the Wolf*, Saint-Saëns's *Carnival of the Animals*, or almost anything by Mozart.**

Sponge Away Boredom

18 Transform a sponge into a squeaky-clean superhero. With suction cups for feet, he's well equipped to cling to a window and ward off a case of the rainy-day blues.

MATERIALS

Glue

2 large googly eyes

Small pom-pom

Small sponge

Permanent marker

2 rubber suction cups

3 pipe cleaners

Craft foam

Ribbon

Glue the googly eyes and a pom-pom nose onto the upper front of the sponge (the type that stays soft when it dries). Use a permanent marker to draw on the mouth.

For legs, remove the metal hooks from the suction cups. Tightly wrap the middle of a pipe cleaner around the knob atop each cup, then twist together the ends of the pipe cleaner, as shown above. Insert the tops of the legs into the bottom of the sponge, using a little glue to secure them.

To make each arm, insert an end of a 4-inch pipe cleaner length into the side of the sponge and use glue to hold it. Next, cut two small ovals out of craft foam and glue them sandwich style onto the end of the arm to create a hand.

Now cut out a craft foam cape. Glue the midsection of a length of ribbon to the upper back edge of the cape. Once the cape is thoroughly dry, tie it onto the sponge just above the arms.

Instant Stickers

19 **Kids can never have too many stickers, and here's a fun way to keep your family well supplied. Cut a bunch of pictures from old magazines, comic books, or gift wrap. Then dissolve 2 tea-** spoons of flavored gelatin in 5 teaspoons of boiling water (adults only). With a small paintbrush, coat the backs of the cutouts with a thin layer of gelatin solution. Let them dry, and the stickers are ready to lick and stick.

Bean Scene

20 Want to see bean soup moonlight glamorously as a mosaic? Have your child arrange a bunch of colorful dried peas and beans into a festive legume collage. To begin, sketch a design on a piece of corrugated cardboard. Next, use a paintbrush to cover a small portion of the design with a thick coat of white glue. Now arrange beans on top of the glued area, following the drawn figures and shapes. Continue gluing beans until the entire design is filled in.

Peanut Pals

21 If you're looking for a quick and easy project to keep your peanut gallery amused, we recommend rounding up a few peanut buddies.

MATERIALS

- **Brown lunch bag**
- **Newspaper or packing peanuts**
- **Tape**
- **Colored markers**
- **Brown paper**
- **Glue**

Stuff the lunch bag with newspaper or, better yet, packing peanuts. Seal the top of the bag with tape, then scrunch the middle so that it resembles the shape of a real peanut. Draw on a face with colored markers. For stalklike arms and legs, accordion-fold brown paper strips and glue them to the body. Lastly, glue peanut-shaped paper feet to the ends of the legs.

FUN FACT The average American eats about 11 pounds of peanuts per year, and most kids will have consumed some 1,500 PB & J's by the time they've graduated from high school.

Bean Soup Relay

22 Ending up with the biggest hill of beans is the goal in this 3-minute relay. For each team, place a bowl filled with dried beans at the starting line, then set a grocery bag 20 feet from each bowl. When the race begins, the first person on each team uses a wooden spoon to scoop up beans from his team's bowl, then races off to dump them in the team bag. He hands off the spoon to the next person, who follows suit, and so on, until the time is up. The team with the most beans in its bag wins.

Pipe-Cleanosaurus

23 This lumbering giant roamed the earth during the Craft-aceous Period, which followed the snack and rest periods.

MATERIALS

- **8 green pipe cleaners**
- **Glue**
- **Googly eyes**

STEP 1: Connect three green pipe cleaners end to end.

STEP 2: Wrap them around a thick marker for the body.

STEP 3: Connect two green pipe cleaners end to end.

STEP 4: Wrap half around a pencil for the head, then coil some for the neck. Leave a 1-inch stem.

STEP 5: Attach the head and neck by inserting the stem into the body. Glue.

STEP 6: For the tail, coil one green pipe cleaner around a pencil, leaving a 1-inch stem.

STEP 7: Insert the attaching stem into the body.

STEP 8: Make legs by bending two green pipe cleaners into V's, then coiling each end around a pencil.

STEP 9: Insert the legs into the body, between the coils. Glue. Glue on googly eyes.

28

Pipe Cleaner People

24 Don't be put off by their twisted appearance: making pipe cleaner humans is a snap. Fortunately for the pipe cleaner sculptor, pipe cleaners come in all colors — just like people.

MATERIALS

- **Pipe cleaners**
- **Fingernail clippers**
- **Glue**
- **Googly eyes**
- **Markers**

STEP 1: Make a V with a pipe cleaner and twist a small loop at the top.

STEP 2: Twist together the two ends a few times to make the torso.

STEP 3: Coil another pipe cleaner around a pencil.

STEP 4: Slide the coil onto the torso.

STEP 5: Clip a pipe cleaner in half with fingernail clippers and slide one half through the loop.

STEP 6: Wrap a pipe cleaner around a pencil and stick it on the loop to make a head.

STEP 7: Make loops at the ends of the arms and legs for hands and feet.

STEP 8: Glue on googly eyes and pipe cleaner accessories: hair (a C-shaped snippet of brown), a necktie (looped from red), and a briefcase (a length of black bent back and forth).

Hunt for Buried Treasure

25 At first glance, this homemade toy may look like nothing more than a bottle of rice, but roll it once or twice and a host of hidden objects will appear before your eyes.

MATERIALS

Clean, clear plastic soda bottle

Assorted trinkets (beads, buttons, charms, plastic insects, dime-store jewelry)

Uncooked rice

Remove the label from the bottle. Gather up the trinkets and put them in the bottle. Add rice to fill the bottle two thirds of the way, then tightly screw on the cap. Shake well to conceal the objects. Now your child can twist and turn the toy to see how many treasures can be spotted inside. **Note:** Heavy objects such as coins and pebbles tend to gravitate into the middle, while lightweight plastic beads, buttons, and trinkets are easier to spot.

No-peeking Sketches

27 With its potential for silliness, this fun drawing game is a great thing to try with your kids. To begin, write the names of a dozen simple items, such as house, dog, plane, and so on, on strips of paper, place the strips in a hat, and have each person take one. Without showing their word to anyone else, players take turns sketching the object with their eyes closed, while the others attempt to guess what is being drawn.

Thread Heads

26 Grab your sewing basket and round up a few of these amusing kooky characters.

To make one, peel away the labels from the top and bottom of a plastic thread spool. Then cut yarn into two dozen 6-inch lengths and divide them into four groups of six. Sandwich each group in a pipe cleaner bent in half. Then fit each set of the pipe cleaner ends into a separate hole in the center of the spool, pulling the ends through just far enough to secure the yarn in place.

When all of the yarn hair is attached, trim four of the pipe cleaner ends protruding from the bottom of the spool so that they are flush with the plastic (a parent's job). Pose the remaining four ends to resemble arms and legs. Finally, glue button eyes and a nose to the thread-covered spool for a face.

Backpack Danglers

28 As any kid will tell you, there's no greater fashion faux pas than a naked backpack. So we devised these jazzy danglers to dress up even the drabbest canvas. You'll need to lay in some inexpensive supplies ahead of time, but once they're handy, your kids can whip up new danglers to suit their daily whims. We've described three methods below, but your kids will undoubtedly dream up their own.

MATERIALS

Narrow ribbon

Buttons with a large threading loop
   on the back

Large safety pins and diaper pins

Elastic cord

Beads

Button Dangler: Fold 8 inches of ribbon in half and thread the loop through the opening of a button. Tie the loose ends in a knot beneath the button to hold it in place. Thread the loop through the closed safety pin, then the button through the loop, as shown above (A).

Diaper Pin Dangler: Fold a 10-inch length of elastic cord in half and loop onto a safety pin, as shown at left (B). Thread beads onto the cord, then knot the cord beneath the last bead. Repeat with three to five more strands.

Bead Dangler (shown at top): Tie a few short lengths of elastic cord onto the circular joint of a safety pin. Thread beads onto the cords, then knot the cords beneath the last bead on each strand.

Bounce a Band Ball

29 Instead of stuffing stray elastics into a desk drawer or (worse!) shooting them across a classroom, your kids can turn them into a bouncy ball with this simple project. To make one, pinch together the ends of a single rubber band and tie it into a loose double knot. Wrap and twist a second band around the knot repeatedly, until it is taut. Continue adding rubber bands one at a time until the ball is as large as you like, or you run out of bands. You also can speed along the process by starting out with an inner core made of wadded-up newspaper or aluminum foil and then covering it with rubber bands.

Friendship Pal

30

Here's a new twist on a summer classic: the friendship bracelet. These dolls are even quicker to make, and they use just one knot, a simple half hitch (see Figure A, below). Kids can make a bunch for their friends and themselves, then pin them to shirts, use them for zipper pulls, or dangle them from their backpacks.

MATERIALS

- **Embroidery floss**
- **Safety pin**
- **Two-hole button**
- **Permanent marker**

1. Cut eight pieces of floss, each about 12 inches long. Hold all the strands together and tie a knot roughly 5 inches from one end (the extra will become hair). Stick the safety pin through the knot and pin it onto your pants

or backpack to make the knotting easier.

2. Separate out two strands on each side for arms. Divide the remaining four strands into two groups (call them pair X and pair Y), which will be knotted to each other to form the body, then knotted individually to form the legs. Begin by holding pair X straight and taut. Loop pair Y over pair X, then send it back up through the loop (as shown in A, below). Pull up the knot to the top and tighten. For the next knot, alternate the strands, holding pair Y straight and taut and sending pair X over and up through the loop. Pull the knot up snugly to the first one. Repeat, alternating sides, until the body is about an inch long.

3. To make the left leg, separate the two strands of pair X and loop one around the other. Continue, but don't alternate sides: simply knot one strand around the other until the leg is about three quarters of an inch long (B). Tie off the ends and trim. Repeat for the right leg and both arms.

4. Attach the button head by running another piece of floss through the buttonholes and knotting it in place above the body (C). Make a hairdo for your pal from the loose ends and draw a face on the button with a permanent marker.

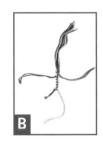
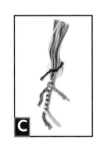

Make Your Mark

Sure, you can color and draw with markers, but what about all the other amazing superpowers they have? Here are some of our favorite marker tips and techniques.

With permanent markers, draw on a balloon, let dry, then inflate it to see the art grow.

Make a drawing with a white crayon, then color over it with a washable marker.

Photocopy a photograph, then colorize it with markers of different colors.

To create a metallic look, draw with permanent markers on a sheet of aluminum foil.

Waiting Games

FUN TO GO

Fun on the Fly

31 Stuck in traffic?

Waiting for your dinner? All it takes is a change of perspective to transform frustration into fun.

Sharpen their wits: Kids love to bet how much, how far, how many. Ask them to guess the number of french fries on your plate, or how quickly you can walk to the car.

Cultivate friendly competition: Want a moment to think? Hold a 5-minute quiet contest. Need to get through your errands in a hurry? Challenge your kids to a race.

Be trivial: Pack questions from a trivia board game in your Emergency Fun Kit (see page 18).

CAR GAME

Bust Backseat Boredom

32 The next time your family is heading out on a road trip, serve up some backseat fun — a tray full of magnetic games and drawing supplies.

MATERIALS

Baking sheet

White dry-erase paper (such as Con-Tact Memoboard)

Magnetic tape

Several dry-erase markers

2-foot length of ribbon

Small cloth square

Plain paper

Buttons

Pocket-style file folder

Cover the cooking surface of the baking sheet with the dry-erase paper to serve as a drawing board. Then affix pieces of magnetic tape to the dry-erase markers. For an eraser, tie one end of the ribbon to the cloth and the other to the hole in the baking sheet handle.

For additional games, draw a checkerboard, crossword puzzles, or bingo-style scorecards of things to look for (a tractor or a horse, for example) on sheets of plain paper. Turn buttons into game pieces by sticking magnetic tape to the backs. To create a handy storage place for your games, apply magnetic tape to the back of a pocket-style file folder and attach it to the back of the baking sheet.

Creative License

33 Here are two imaginative games that'll give you great mileage.

Tally It Up: The object of this contest is to find license plates that have duplicate numbers or letters. The first person to call one out receives a point for each duplicate. For example, the license plate BABY OYL is worth 4 points since it has two *B*'s and two *Y*'s. The person who accumulates the most points wins the game.

A Car of a Different Color: Have everyone predict how many blue cars you will pass in 5 miles. The one who comes closest gets to name a new color to watch for.

Play It in the Car

34 When your kids have asked "Are we there yet?" one too many times, challenge them to a game.

Raindrop Race: Each player traces the course of a raindrop down the window on a parked car. The first drop to hit bottom wins.

Car Scavenger Hunt: Before the trip, hand your kids index cards and ask them to draw pictures of 50 things they might see on the road. Keep the cards for hunts in which players vie to match what they see with the cards.

Waiting for Dinner

It's hard to wait for dinner, and it's even harder to make dinner — especially with a bunch of kids hanging around turning "when" into a four-syllable question. Remember: hungry busy kids are happier than hungry bored kids.

Hire sous-chefs: Kids love to help in the kitchen, and certain tasks are just right for tiny hands. Let them tear lettuce for salad, measure ingredients, or roll meatballs.

Hunt for supper: Each player gets a couple of old magazines, a pair of kiddie scissors, a glue stick, and a paper plate. The object of the game is to find what you're making for dinner. The first player to cut out and glue down pictures of everything you're serving wins.

Make mosaics: Give each child a cracker spread with cream cheese and a bowl of raisins, peanuts, or frozen vegetables and have them create (and eat!) edible mosaics while they wait.

KITCHEN PROJECTS

Play With Your Food

35 A certain Mister seems to have cornered the spud-toy market, but your kids can try our low-tech version for a starchy blast from the past.

MATERIALS

> Baking potatoes
>
> Toothpicks
>
> Assorted edible art materials, such as
>> carrot sticks, cherry tomatoes, parsley
>> sprigs, broccoli florets, olives, and cuke
>> and pepper slices

Have your kids wash their hands and then use the toothpicks to stick the decorative edibles to the blank face of the potato. They can try olive eyes, a cherry tomato nose, parsley hair — whatever sparks their imaginations. They can reuse the same potato for a number of personality changes. When they're done, you can toss any leftover veggies into a salad and boil up the poked spuds to make mashed potatoes.

You can vary this activity according to your dinner plans. If you're making macaroni, let them string necklaces. Slicing carrots? Give the kids an ink pad so they can make circle stamps.

Family Centerpiece

36 What do you do when your kids and your dinner preparations demand equal time? Busy the kids with our dinner-table centerpiece.

MATERIALS

- Old family photos (doubles, duds, or anything you're willing to part with)
- Construction paper
- Pipe cleaners, cut into assorted lengths
- White glue
- Markers or glitter glue (optional)
- Flower vase
- Florist's foam or Styrofoam (optional)

Have your kids cut faces from the photos. The faces will form the flower centers, so they should be roughly circular and about an inch in diameter.

Fold a piece of construction paper in half, then trace several flower shapes on one of the folded sides. Cut out the flowers (you should have two matching shapes for each flower). Create leaves as well.

For each flower, lay one flower shape on your work surface, then lay a pipe cleaner over it so that an inch of the pipe cleaner is on the flower. Spread white glue around the paper edges, then press the matching flower shape on top. Using the same method, glue paper leaves onto pipe cleaners and twist them around the stem. Glue a photo to the center of each flower, then, if desired, decorate the petals with markers or glitter glue.

If you're using florist's foam or Styrofoam, cut it to fit neatly in the container (a grown-up's job) and have your child poke her bouquet into the base. Or simply place the buds in a vase.

Wacky Fun

Blow Bubbles

38 Need some good, clean fun for your kids and their friends? Just mix up a batch of our tried-and-true bubble solution, twist a few pipe cleaners into homemade wands, and try your luck at a couple of bubble tricks on the next page.

INGREDIENTS

3 cups water

1 cup dishwashing liquid

⅓ cup light corn syrup

In a large plastic container, stir the water, dishwashing liquid, and corn syrup. (Although you can use any brand of dish detergent, we found that Joy and Dawn produce the best bubbles.) Store the homemade soap in a covered container. When your kids are ready for some bubble-making fun, make a few homemade wands, following the directions on the next page. **Tip:** The best time to blow bubbles is when the air is calm and muggy, such as after a rain shower (bubbles last longer when there's more humidity).

FUN FACT The longest bubble was 105 feet long, created with a wand and homemade soap by Alan McKay of New Zealand.

TRY THIS NOW

How to Blow a Double Bubble

39 Here's a trick from bubble-ologist Casey Carle (www.bubblemania.com). 1. Balance a bubble on your wand. 2. Wet the bottom two thirds of a straw in bubble solution. 3. Poke the straw through the side of the bubble until the straw's end is in the bubble's center (wetting the straw keeps the bubble from popping). Blow gently!

Make Tiny Bubbles

40 For a slew of miniature bubbles, tape together a bunch of plastic drinking straws, as shown in the photo at left. Dip one end in the bubble solution, hold the other about 1 inch from your mouth (do not put your lips on the straws), and blow.

Bubble Magic

41 Need an ice-breaker for a summer party? Set out a pie plate filled with home-made bubble soap (see recipe on the previous page), try these two tricks, and your guests will be bubbling over in no time.

Poke it: Blow a bubble and catch it in your hand. Stick one finger into a cup of water and then immediately through the top of the bubble. It won't pop!

Hand it over: See if you can catch one bubble in your palm. The trick is to dip your hand in the soapy solution first, since it's dryness, not sharpness, that usually bursts a bubble. Then try passing it to someone else.

Homemade Wonder Wands

42 When you're creating something magical, the right wand is crucial (just ask Harry Potter). Here are a few good ones — from mini to monster — all made from household items.

MINIATURE PAPER CLIP WAND

How to make it: Bend a paper clip into a bubble wand shape. **Dipping container:** Cap from a small jar. **What you'll get:** A single baby bubble.

FLYSWATTER BUBBLETTE WAND

How to make it: Grab a clean fly-swatter. **Dipping container:** Flying disk turned upside down. **What you'll get:** Cumulus-cloudlike masses of mini bubbles.

CLASSIC COAT HANGER WAND

How to make it: Bend a hanger into a circle and handle. Wrap the circle with string. **Dipping container:** Upside-down trash can lid. **What you'll get:** A *looong* bubble.

GIANT HULA WAND

How to make it: Dig out your hula hoop. **Dipping container:** Kiddie pool (hold hoop as shown above). **What you'll get:** Say aloha to the biggest bubbles ever.

String Knot

43 Your mission? To tie a knot in a 2-foot-long string without letting go with either hand. It's a cinch if you cross your arms first and then pick up the string by both ends. Next, uncross your arms, and you'll automatically knot the string.

Doorway Liftoff

45 Here's a fun way to get a rise out of your child. Ask him to stand in a doorway with his arms at his sides. Then have him press his arms outward, so that the backs of his hands and wrists push against the door frame, for a full minute. Next, have him quickly step forward out of the doorway. What happens? His arms will seem to float up and away of their own accord!

Why? While he stood in the doorway, his arms became accustomed to pressing out against the resistance of the door frame. Once he stepped out of the doorway, his arms were still trying to press outward, and with no door frame to hold them back, away they went.

Hole-in-one Relay

44 In this game, players have to pucker up for a sticky pass-off. The object is to pass a Life Savers candy from teammate to teammate using only drinking straws held between their teeth.

MATERIALS

Plastic drinking straws

Life Savers candies

First, cut a bunch of straws into halves and give one to each player. Then ask teammates to line up side by side with everyone holding their half straws between their lips, keeping their arms behind their backs. Slip a Life Saver (alternatively, you can try using rigatoni noodles and straws, or even doughnuts and chopsticks) onto the straw belonging to the first person in each line.

When the relay starts, players try to slide their team's candy from straw to straw (remember, no hands allowed) all the way down the line and then back again. If a candy gets dropped along the way, that team must start again from the beginning of the line. The first group to complete the task wins.

MORE WACKY FUN Still looking for a silly game? Line up plastic cups in the Bowling Pin Derby on page 84 or hop across the carpet in the Penguin Games on page 85.

Shadow Show

46 Looking for a bit of fun before the sun goes down? Invite your kids to join in some shadow fun and games.

Dancing shadows: Pair up and, keeping the beat to a familiar tune, see if you can make your shadows clap hands without your real hands actually touching.

Hold a shadow race: Line up all the contestents with the sun at their backs so that the heads of their shadows are just behind the starting line (taller kids may need to stand a bit farther back than shorter children). The person whose shadow crosses the finish line first wins.

Martian Mallow Meltdown

47 It's an alien! It's a s'more! Actually, it's both, made with just a few scissor snips and a blast of "radiation" in the microwave.

1. Snip a marshmallow into a triangular head and another into a torso with arms. Insert mini chocolate chip eyes.

2. Assemble the Martian Mallow on a chocolate "flying saucer" wafer. Place him in your nuclear transporter (microwave).

3. Ten seconds on high, and he's s'morphed! After he cools down, let him visit Planet Mouth.

Crawl Like a Crocodile

48 When a crocodile races across land, it drops onto its belly and weaves from side to side, moving all four legs as fast as it can. Your kids can get up to croc speed in this wriggly challenge. The game starts with three or more players lying on their bellies, about 5 feet apart from one another. The object is to wiggle across the floor (tummy touching) and tag all of the other players with your hand before they tag you.

Instant Fun

The Flamingo Stance Dance

49 At your child's next sleep-over party, try this game. Have kids pair off and stand facing one another. They then put their hands on one another's shoulders, and each attempts to balance on one leg while wrapping the other around his or her partner's leg. The object: to keep your balance longer than the other pairs can.

Connect the Clips

50 You don't need to be a magician to dazzle people with this trick — you just need a 3- by 12-inch strip of paper and two paper clips. **1.** First, curve one end of the paper strip toward you and fasten it in place with one paper clip. **2.** Next, curve the other end of the strip away from you and fasten it to the back of the first loop with the other paper clip. **3.** Now you are ready to perform the trick. Hold the two ends of the strip in your hands, say the magic word (*abracadabra*, of course), and quickly pull the ends in opposite directions. Quicker than the eye can see, the clips should connect and fly off the paper (if not, keep trying).

Step on Paper Bag Stones

51 Instead of making a bee-line to the finish, contestants in this race hop, skip, or jump down a path of stepping-stones.

MATERIALS

Large brown bags

Markers

For each child, fold and flatten two bags to make a pair of stepping-stones. Trace a pair of the child's feet on each bag, and let him color in his footprints with markers. Players then line up side by side while standing on one of their stones. On cue, each child drops his other stone on the floor in front of him and leaps onto it. Keeping at least one foot in place, he then picks up his first stone, tosses it ahead of him, makes the jump, and so on. If at any time a player does not land on a stone, he must go back one step. First one to cross the finish wins.

Feather Vault

53 All it takes is a feather for each child to get this event under way — or airborne. (You can buy a package of feathers at many department stores or hobby shops.) On cue, players try to blow their feathers overhead. Whoever keeps one aloft the longest without using any hands is the winner. For a team challenge, kids can pair up and face each other from a distance of 3 feet, then try to volley a feather between them.

Yo-yo Tricks

54 Master these three tricks and you'll soon be a spin doctor.

The Sleeper: Hold the yo-yo in your hand, palm up. Sharply flip your wrist over, sending the yo-yo forward, arcing over your index finger. Let it spin at the bottom of the string, then tug it to make it return.

Up and Over: Snap off a Sleeper, then carefully work your elbow underneath the string (like you're shouldering a sack). Jerk your arm so the yo-yo travels up, over, and down in front of you.

Walk the Dog: Send your yo-yo into a fast Sleeper, then gingerly lower it to the ground (a carpeted area works best). Give the yo-yo slack as it scoots ahead, then give it a tug.

Spin a Whirligig

52 This Colonial spinning toy was popular when George Washington was a tot. Here's how you and your kids can make your own 18th-century spinning whirligig.

MATERIALS

Corrugated cardboard

Markers

String

To make this simple toy, cut out a 4-inch circle from the corrugated cardboard. With markers, draw a spiral design on both sides of the disk, then poke two small holes in the middle (about ¾ inch apart). Thread a 2-foot-long string through the holes and tie it to form a loop.

Keeping the disk in the middle, hold the string on both sides and spin the whirligig like a jump rope to wind the string tightly. To make it whirl, gently pull and relax the string. **Hint:** Move your hands in and out as if you were playing an accordion to keep the disk spinning.

41

CHAPTER THREE

Backyard Games

Our favorite lawn, pool, and blacktop games are a snap to learn — and will motivate even the busiest families to come out and play

Growing up in a family of nine, *FamilyFun* backyard expert John Porcino always looked forward to those summer evenings when the kids could persuade Mom or Dad to play outside with them after dinner. Whether the game was kickball or kick the can, charades or flashlight tag, those lingering summer hours in the backyard remain some of his happiest memories. "These days after dinner, it's *my* shirt that gets tugged on by kids, specifically by my son and daughter and their neighborhood friends," John tells us. They know that John's collected quite a pocketful of games, having worked as a camp director, teacher, and storyteller. "Some evenings, my thoughts lean more toward a lounge chair and the newspaper," John admits, "but then I recall the delight I felt as a child and try to dig out a game or two."

The following games include some of the Porcino family's favorites — and a host of other popular games from the pages of *FamilyFun* magazine. Like the best backyard classics, they require little or no equipment, are easy to learn, and can be played by groups of all sizes. Ever adaptable, they serve equally well as a 5-minute diversion before bathtime or as an entire day's entertainment, ended only by the sounds of parents calling in their reluctant kids through the darkness.

Playing simple outdoor games with friends and family does more than just pass the time. Kids huff and puff and get into shape without realizing that's what they're doing. And, as John points out, "It lets us rediscover a bit of childhood's magic." That's something to keep in mind next time you too feel the tug.

Allow us to offer some homespun backyard coaching:

Play along with your kids. Kids and parents have been playing games together as long as there have been backyards and Saturdays. But for the

Chalk games, page 67

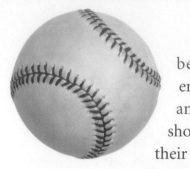

best experience, parents and children should give up their usual roles and let the pure fun of the game take over. Laugh a lot, be silly, and enjoy the fresh air.

Change the rules to suit your audience. When playing games with your kids, it's important to adapt the games to their ages and abilities. If your child is ten, for instance, tailor the rules to the skill level of a ten-year-old.

Don't be the referee. Acting as an umpire or coach will put you above the kids, not bring you closer. Even well-meaning advice can spoil the fun of playing the game. So let the kids decide the teams and the rules.

Make time for time-outs. During high-action games, designate a safe spot (you can call it the Clinic) for kids feeling a bit tired, roughed up, or out of breath. A shady patch of grass, a blanket to sit on, or the top of a cooler all work fine. Provide a large water bottle. The point is to create a refuge, especially for the little ones who want to join in the play (although we've seen plenty of teenagers head there for a cooldown as well).

Store your equipment at kid level. Set up a system for storing balls, rackets, and other backyard playthings that helps your kids find what they want, when they want it.

One family we know lines up inexpensive plastic garbage cans in the garage to hold all kinds of sports equipment. A trash can full of balls is right next to another that holds baseball bats and hockey sticks.

Teach sportsmanship. Playing games can teach kids important — perhaps even difficult — lessons about winning, losing, and trying their best. Remind your kids to praise opponents who make a good play — and to shake hands and say, "Nice game," whoever wins.

Remember that fun comes first. Kids are into games for the fun, the excitement, the participation, and to be with their friends. So when the game is over, don't ask your kids if they won; instead ask, "Did you have fun?"

Backyard Classics

Considering all the backyard games kids have played over the centuries, you'd think we'd never be at a loss for something fun to play. But standing in the twilight with a group of kids milling about, it's all too easy to forget the classics. Here's a reminder:

* Simon says
* Duck, duck, goose
* Red light, green light
* Mother, may I?
* Red rover
* Hopscotch
* Sardines
* Kick the can
* Dodgeball
* Pickle/running bases
* Spud (see page 48)
* Capture the flag
* Frisbee golf (below)

Ball Games

Ready, Set, Go!

With a stopwatch and a bit of imagination, your kids can clock hours of kooky contests.

+ **How many baskets can you shoot in 2 minutes?**

+ **How long does it take to blow a perfect bubble after you put a new piece of gum in your mouth?**

+ **How long does it take to run around the house?**

+ **How many times can you snap your fingers in a minute?**

Backyard Games

TRAINING GAME

Soccer Dodgeball

55 Many classic kids' games make great training games for your young athletes. Kids can try their hands — or feet! — at this version of dodgeball. Instead of throwing the ball, you kick it.

WHAT YOU NEED

Soccer ball

4 to 6 players

Have the kids form a ring with one kid in the center. The outside players take turns shooting at the player on the inside, who's scrambling to avoid the ball. Whoever hits the target player gets to take his or her place. Watch to make sure players keep their kicks low.

FUN FACT In a typical soccer game, players run as many as 4 to 6 miles.

Football Defender

56 A football and a grassy field can add up to hours of good, sweaty fun. After playing a few rounds of touch football, try this twist.

WHAT YOU NEED

Football

3 players

Defender is a pass-and-catch game, with a quarterback and receiver matching up against a defensive back. For young kids, a shorter, narrower field works best. The object is to move down the field and score a touchdown, but the offense can proceed only by completing passes; there's no running with the ball after the catch (and thus no tackling). Three completions make a first down. If the offense fails to complete the three passes in a four-down series, the players switch positions — quarterback to receiver, receiver to defender, and defender to QB — and play marches back down the field in the opposite direction. An interception automatically entitles the defender to switch places with the quarterback.

Goal Tending

"To help mark our achievements and keep the creative juices flowing, our family has come up with a special goals chart for our refrigerator. Each family member (my husband and me, Lindsey, age eight, Alex, five, and Eric, one) writes (or has someone help him or her write) a goal on a paper football — everything from 'learn to juggle' to 'learn to tie my shoes.' The footballs are dated and signed on the back, then taped to the refrigerator near a construction paper goalpost. When one of us reaches a goal, we move that football between the goalposts and celebrate with a special dinner or outing."

— Kathy Bias, Alpharetta, Georgia

Chase the Dog

57 All you need is a basketball and a bandanna tucked into each player's pocket (to resemble a tail) to get this group game started. While staying within a designated area and continually dribbling their balls, players try to grab each other's bandannas. As soon as a player loses his tail, he is out. The game continues until only one child, the top dog, is left with his tail.

TRAINING GAME

King of the Dribblers

58 If your kids tire of straight-up one-on-one, let them try another driveway classic.

WHAT YOU NEED

Basketball

5 or more players

Young kids tend to look down at the ball when they dribble. Here's a game that will break them of this habit.

Designate or cone off an area (less skilled kids need a bigger area). Everyone gets a ball. Players must stay inside the area and dribble; no standing around. As they bounce the ball, they try to knock everyone else's ball away with their free hand. When a player's ball gets knocked outside the designated area, he or she is out. The last player dribbling is crowned king or queen. After right-handed dribbling, try left-handed.

Laundry Hoop

We all know the anatomy of a peeled-off outfit — that bedside heap of dirty-kneed jeans topped by an inside-out T-shirt/ sweatshirt combo. Becky Sprague, a mother of four from Richmond, Indiana, knew it all too well. Backed by the if-you-can't-lick-'em-join-'em philosophy, she installed a basketball hoop hung with a laundry-bag net. The hoop is a yard sale find screwed to her sons' bedroom wall. The net is a mesh laundry bag with a zipper closing. She cut open the bottom and hooked the bag to the rim, zipper end down. When laundry day comes, she places her basket beneath the full bag and opens the zipper. Score!

Baseball Cupcake

59 For a grand-slam gameside treat, decorate a batch of cupcakes to look like baseballs. First, frost each cupcake with white icing. Using the stitching of a real baseball as your guide, re-create the pattern with red shoe-string licorice (or with red frosting and a writing tip). With chocolate frosting and a writing tip, have the kids sign the ball with the name of their favorite player.

PLAYGROUND GAMES

Bounce a Red Ball

60 Red balls are kinder and gentler than basketballs and easier to throw than footballs — making them the perfect choice for younger children.

WHAT YOU NEED

Red playground ball

Chalk

2 players

Feat Ball: Contestants in this game take turns tossing a ball against a cement wall and catching it before it hits the ground. What's the hitch? Before making a catch, a player must complete a task posed by the challenger. For example, the first child might pitch the ball at the wall and clap his hands together before making the catch. The second player then tries to accomplish the same feat. If successful, he gets to pose the next challenge — perhaps tapping his shoulders or spinning around before catching the ball. If he fails, the first player earns 1 point and gets to pose a second challenge. The first one to score 5 points wins the game.

Bull's-eye Bounce: Draw a 5-foot-wide chalk circle on the ground about 10 feet from a cement wall. Draw a 2-foot-wide inner circle in the center. Players take turns tossing a rubber ball at the wall and letting it bounce on the ground once before catching it. If the ball lands on the center circle before a player catches it, he earns 10 points; if it bounces in the outer ring, he earns 5 points. The first child whose score totals 50 points is the winner.

Spud

61 Here's our favorite version of this time-honored recess game. Everyone counts off and stands with one foot on a designated base. The player who is "It" throws the ball high in the air and calls out one player's number. As the other players scatter, the called player tries to grab the ball. When he does, he shouts "Spud!" at which point the other players must freeze. The ball holder can take two giant steps toward any person, whom he then tries to hit with the ball. The target person can evade the throw by moving his body but not his feet. If the thrower misses or the target catches the ball, the thrower earns an *S.* If he hits the target, that person earns an *S.* Whoever earns the letter becomes It and tosses the ball to start the next round. Players are eliminated once they earn S-P-U-D. Last person still in the game wins.

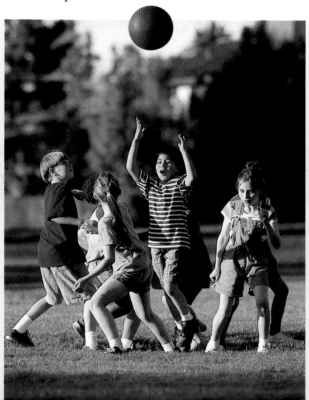

48

Olympic Party

For her son Jackson's sixth birthday, Barbara Graydon of Columbus, Georgia, planned an Olympic party, complete with games, a medal ceremony, and for decorations, 20 international flags. This sweet Olympic finale really took the cake! "That was the best birthday party ever!" decreed the joyful Olympian.

KID CLASSIC

Play Four Square

62
No keeping score, no winner, and still the best darn game at recess.

WHAT YOU NEED

> Red playground ball
>
> Chalk
>
> 4 players

Classic four square: Draw the four-square court with chalk, as shown. The player in box 1 bounces and serves the ball. The others must let it bounce in their box before hitting it into another. When a player muffs it, he moves to box 4 (or to the end of the line waiting at box 4), and the others players rotate up toward box 1.

Advanced four square: In advanced four square, you add in all sorts of variations, which are called out by the server. Each command stops the action, and players must place their feet in a specific place. The last to do so is out. Try these — Bus stop: All must step on the outer corner of their square. Fire alarm: All must jump out of their square. Mailbox: All must step in the middle where the two lines meet. Big tomato: All must do a mailbox and then a fire alarm. Around the world colors: When players bounce the ball, they must also call out a color — or state, animal, pizza topping — whatever the category may be (no repeating). Normal: Play goes back to, you guessed it, normal.

Tags & Relays

The Stuff-stacle Course

63 With a bit of imagination, a bunch of old toys and sporting goods can speedily transform a seemingly boring backyard into a magnificent Stuff-stacle Course.

WHAT YOU NEED

Stuff

A stopwatch or a watch with a second hand

1 to 10 players

The idea here is to rig your stuff into an instant obstacle course. Go to your garage and dig out that old tricycle, Styrofoam swimming noodles, a pair of hula hoops, and eight winter hats you've not yet put away.

Consider it all, size up the yard, and — voilà! — the UnExtreme Games. Time the kids as they whoosh down your playground slide; wiggle through the hula hoops you've strung from a branch; sprint around an eight-hat slalom course; hurdle over the noodles, propped on overturned plastic garbage pails; crazily ride the tricycle to the garage … you get the picture. Make your own course and keep it up for a few days. Try completing it backward. Why not create a personal best chart? Then see if you can beat your top time. **Tip:** Think safety when you set up the course; there's a lot to trip over here.

Friend Tag

64 This version of tag takes the loneliness out of being "It." Two players link hands and become the taggers, chasing after the other players. When the taggers tag someone, that player becomes part of the team. Play continues until all the players are linked.

On Your Mark, Get Set, Blow!

65 Got a pack of gum chums? Try this relay at your next party. Divide into two teams and have each team form a line. The first person in line runs over to a pile of bubble gum, unwraps and chews a piece, and blows a bubble as quickly as possible. Once a judge has seen a legit bubble, the next person in line does the same. The first team to finish wins!

Octopus Tag

66 A cross between red rover and tag, this is a game the neighborhood kids can play over and over.

WHAT YOU NEED

Clothing or other markers to delineate your ocean

6 or more players

Set up a rectangular ocean: to determine the right width, have everyone hold hands and spread out across the field. Indicate the two sidelines with clothing or other markers. The fish line up at one end; the queen (or king) octopus stands in the middle and cries out, "I am the octopus, queen of all motion. Let's see if you can cross my ocean." The fish try to run or sneak across the ocean as the octopus tries to tag them. If tagged, they become seaweed. Keeping one foot planted, the seaweed try to reach out and tag the fish running by, thus turning those players into seaweed too. Once the fish reach the other side, the octopus and seaweed say the chant, and the crossing contest starts again. The game continues until all the fish become seaweed. The last fish tagged becomes the new octopus.

Sneaker Relay

67 This wacky team relay begins with everyone wearing sneakers. Divide into teams and set up a box or bin across from each one at the far end of a level grassy area. On cue, the first person in each group races to his team's box, removes and deposits his shoes, then runs back to tag the next person. The game continues in this way until the last teammate in line has thrown his shoes in the box and has run back across the starting line. Then the first person races back to the box to retrieve his shoes and put them on before retagging the next person, and so on. The team whose members are first to complete both parts of the relay wins.

KITCHEN FUN

Edible Medals

68 If you want to make victory truly sweet, award these gold medals made from cookies to all of the players in your backyard games. To make one, just seal a sugar cookie in plastic wrap, then wrap it in a circle of gold wrapping paper (leave a wide border around the cookie when you cut out your circle). Wrap tightly and tape. Finally, tape a paper clip to the back for a hanging loop and thread through a yard of red, white, and blue ribbon. Knot the ends of the ribbon, and the medals will disappear in record time!

Easy-as-pie Tag

69 No matter how you slice it, this pie-shaped grid is all it takes to start a lively round of tag. On a level playing surface, draw (use chalk on blacktop or a stick in the dirt) a circle that is at least 15 to 20 feet wide. Then divide the circle into six equal sections by drawing three lines across its center. Now you're ready to play. The player who is chosen to be "It" stands in the center of the circle (where the slices of the pie meet). The remaining players position themselves around the outer edge. To begin, It yells "Go!" and then chases after the other players in an attempt to tag one. The runners may travel in any direction around the circle to avoid being tagged. But here's the catch: their feet must always land on a line. The first person to be tagged, or to step off a line, becomes the new It.

FUN FACT The first Olympians were awarded no metal medals! Instead, these ancient sports stars were crowned with wreaths crafted from the branches of an olive tree.

COOL-OFF GAME

Soggy Jog Relay

70 Put on your swimsuits and start running in this wet and wild relay.

WHAT YOU NEED

Soft, grassy area to run on

Pair of loose-fitting sweatpants for each team

Large bucket of water

Lawn chair

1 to 10 players

Line up the teams side by side, set the bucket of water between them, and position the lawn chair 20 feet away. At the signal, the first child in each line dunks his team's sweatpants into the water, puts them on, and then runs around the chair and back to the starting line. There, he peels off the sweatpants (like a banana) and gives them to the next runner to dunk and don (inside out or right side out), and so on. The first team whose members have all completed the task wins.

Smuggle the Gold

72 A great variation on classic tag, the aim of this game is to get rid of the treasure. It's a challenge for even the most accomplished playground athlete. The twist is that no one knows who's "It" but It himself.

WHAT YOU NEED

Small object to be the gold (this can be anything from a marble to a small plastic toy)

5 to 10 players

First, explain that whoever is holding the gold is the smuggler. Then it's time to secretly slip the gold into one kid's hand. To do so, conceal the gold in your fist and walk from child to child pretending to put the gold in each person's hand. Somewhere along the way, you'll need to actually transfer the gold to one of the players, at which time he should act nonchalant. Continue pretending to transfer the gold to a few more players before announcing that you no longer have the gold. Then start the game by shouting "Smugglers, ahoy!"

Everyone now tries to run from everyone else because anyone could be the smuggler. Each player tries to tag another player before he is tagged himself. If tagged, a player must hold out her hand and discreetly accept whatever the tagger has to offer. If it's nothing, both players resume running. If a player gets the gold, he or she secretly becomes the new smuggler.

Homemade Gelatin Pops

71 Nothing cools you down after a steamy summer game like a frozen pop — especially one you made yourself just a few hours before.

To make the pops, mix 1 small package of flavored gelatin and 1/3 cup of sugar in a large bowl. Add 1 cup of boiling water (adults only) and stir until the mixture is dissolved. Stir in 1 1/3 cups of cold water. Pour into molds or cups and freeze for about 4 hours. You can use either store-bought plastic ice-pop molds or plain old paper cups (the smallest size works best). Here's a trick for the latter: to keep your craft stick handles

centered in the pop, cover the cups with aluminum foil and insert the craft sticks through the covering. To remove the pop from the mold, briefly run the mold under hot tap water. Fills 6 ice-pop molds or about 10 small paper cups.

Water Fun

My Cup Runneth Over

73 Set up a sprinkler on a hot day, and your kids may even forget about that built-in pool you promised. When they tire of running through the sprinkler, challenge them to this simple game. Two players or teams stand on opposite sides of an oscillating sprinkler. When the sheet of water passes into his or her side, each player tries to be the first to completely fill a cup or yogurt container. Here's the catch: you have to keep both feet planted. If you take a step trying to get that extra drop (or to avoid a spray in the face), you have to dump out your cup on your own head. **Variation:** Players gather around the perimeter of an impact sprinkler (the *tick-tick-tick, fttttttttwp* kind) and, without moving their feet, try to fill a cup as the stream of water passes by.

Spray That Funky Music

74 Kids love to make noise and use a hose. You need the lawn and garden watered. With this activity, everyone wins.

WHAT YOU NEED

Garden hose

Musical stuff (inflated beach balls, old hubcaps, aluminum pie pans, metal colanders)

String

Help your child hang a collection of items along a fence or row of bushes, using string or other means to secure them. Next, let the kids blast them, one by one, with a nozzled garden hose (with much of the water, of course, hitting the lawn and bushes below) for a medley of distinctive percussive sounds.

Car Wash Sponge Relay

75 Split players into two teams. Give each team a car-washing sponge and set up two identical buckets at the far end of the pool. The first player from each team swims across the pool holding the sponge and trying to saturate it as much as possible. Upon reaching the other side of the pool, each swimmer squeezes out the sponge into her team's bucket. The players then swim back to pass the sponge to the next person on their team. After everyone has had a turn, measure the water level in each bucket by standing a ruler inside; the team with the most water wins.

Backyard Games

Pool Cake

76 When *FamilyFun* reader Gail Fournier's son, Scott, turned seven, she was hot on throwing a poolside bash. The coolest part of the party was the cake, modeled after the aboveground pool in their New Hampshire backyard. When we tested Gail's recipe, we frosted a 9-inch round layer cake, put on fudge-stick siding, topped it with blue frosting waves, and decorated it with plastic swimmers, gummy-ring inner tubes, Gobstopper beach balls, a licorice ladder, and paper umbrellas. When it was time to taste-test, the kids, like Scott's party guests, had no difficulty taking the plunge.

Frosty Free-for-all

77 Counting your cubes before they melt is the key to success in this cool-off game. For each team, nestle a large plastic bowl or a small pail in the center of an inflated pool doughnut and set it afloat in the pool. Once everyone's in the water, dump a large bag or two of ice cubes into the center of the pool. The team that gets the most cubes in its bucket within 3 minutes wins.

Dive for Correct Change

78 Young swimmers love the challenge of diving for coins. Now, with goggles and a fistful of change, you can test their underwater dexterity and their math skills at the same time. And you thought you'd never find a use for those Sacagawea dollar coins!

WHAT YOU NEED

Swimming pool

1 to 4 players

Coins

Throw the change into the pool and ask your aquanauts to bring back, say, 17 cents. For older kids, challenge them with a figure like $1.27.

Sea Horse Noodle Race

81 For a wacky pool race, have kids ride noodle floats like sea horses. They should sit on them like jockeys and paddle to the other side of the pool.

QUICK COOL-OFF

Hydro High Jump

79 The quickest way to beat the heat on a sultry day is to get wet. While the best method may be up for debate, this watery reverse limbo is a strong contender.

WHAT YOU NEED

Garden hose

2 to 10 players

Spray a long, thin horizontal stream of water 6 inches above the ground. Have everyone line up as you would for limbo and explain that instead of going under the water, the aim is to jump over it without getting wet. Whoever succeeds advances to the next round, in which the hose is raised by another 6 inches, and so on, until only one contestant remains dry and wins.

Variation: Do the water limbo. Hold the hose so the water arcs and your kids can shimmy underneath it. (This game works best when accompanied by snappy calypso music.)

KID CLASSIC

Spray-bottle Capture the Flag

80 To play this water version of the classic camp game, divide everyone into two teams. Each must defend a flag (a water balloon) while trying to capture (and stomp on) the opposing team's. Instead of tagging opposing players to "freeze" them, you squirt them with a spray bottle. To release teammates from a freeze, you have to squirt them again!

Backyard Games

QUICK COOL-OFF

Water Squirtball

82

In this one-on-one water showdown, players win points by squirting a beach ball over an opponent's goal line. You can use soaker-type squirt guns or — for a more serious session — garden hoses with pistol-type nozzles, as we show here. (If you have just one spigot, divide your main hose with a Y connector, then attach two other hoses and nozzles.) Designate two end zones in the yard using cones, Frisbees, lawn chairs, or what-have-you. Each player takes a nozzle, the ref turns on the water, and the players try to blast the beach ball over their opponent's goal line while preventing the ball from crossing their own.

Cool Pool Games

83 To make a day at the pool with friends go swimmingly, invite the kids to try their luck at the following cool-off games. (Of course, make sure each contest is supervised.)

WHAT YOU NEED

Newspaper

Balloons or Ping-Pong balls

2 to 8 players

Dry-run Derby: Have the kids line up at the shallow end of the pool, then hand each one a dry sheet of newspaper (you can also use dry washcloths or paper towels for this game). On cue, everyone enters the water and starts swimming while holding their papers above the water. The goal is to deliver the driest paper to the opposite end of the pool.

Balloon Push: The object of this contest is to race to the far end of the pool while pushing a balloon with your nose. For each swimmer, fill a balloon with about ⅛ cup of water, then blow it up the rest of the way and knot it. The water will weigh down the balloon enough so that it will float atop the water without blowing away. (You can substitute corks, Ping-Pong balls, or other suitable buoyant objects.)

QUICK CRAFT

Foil Fleet

84 Gently pinch one end of a mini aluminum foil loaf pan to shape the bow, then press a small lump of clay onto the center of the boat. Thread a triangular sail (cut from flexible vinyl) onto a bamboo skewer and insert it into the clay. Tie fishing line to the boat and set sail!

FAMILYFUN READER IDEA

On Ice

"A few summers ago, when it was so hot that our swimming pool felt more like a bathtub, I came up with a cool idea for a pool toy. I used baking pans to freeze large rectangles of ice. Once in the pool, these ice blocks not only helped to cool things down, they also provided great entertainment" — Julie Miller, Arlington, Texas

QUICK COOL-OFF

Grease a Watermelon

85 This silly pastime is a hallowed tradition at summer camps. To play, divide everyone into two teams. Each defends a goal, either a dock or one side of a swimming pool. Players enter the water, and the melon – made slippery with vegetable shortening – is floated out into the center of the playing area. At a signal, each team attempts to maneuver the melon toward the other team's goal and heft it up onto dry land. The winners get to split the melon; the losers get to beg.

Lawn Games

Mower Mazes

"In southern Florida, the grass grows very fast, especially in the summertime. One of our favorite things to do is make mower mazes in the backyard. As I mow in rows, I stop and restart the blades to make paths that begin and end randomly and that sometimes cross and loop around. After I head to the front lawn with the mower, my two sons, Luke, age eight, and Leigh, seven, love to run around and find their way to the designated end — usually the swings or the sandbox. The time the boys spend playing in the backyard gives me an opportunity to mow the front yard without interruption."

— Lori Waters, Homestead, Florida

WACKY FUN

Play Crazy Croquet

86 A cross between miniature golf, that gaudy vacation favorite, and croquet, its more mannerly cousin, this game is sure to keep kids giggling across the green.

WHAT YOU NEED

Mallets and balls from a croquet set

Assorted objects for obstacles

Create a crazy course with objects you have on hand. Instead of wickets (which can be difficult for kids to aim for) try setting up simple targets and obstacles. Perhaps the ball has to roll under the slide of your swing set, or between the wheels of a trike. Or it has to bump a large stuffed giraffe before tapping your pink flamingo lawn ornament. Picnic tables, sawhorses, spare tires: see how much of your stuff you can get into action to make your course as full and varied as possible. You can also cut large, arched openings into cardboard boxes, or make ball-guiding bumpers by lining up two rows of bricks.

Before you begin, agree on a clear course through the "wickets" and on any other silly rules you may want to add (a song that you have to sing before you swing, maybe, or hopping on one foot over to your ball). **Tip:** If the mallets are too hard to manage, teach kids how to safely throw the ball (underhand) at a low height.

Stumps

87 The strongest in the family might think they'll rule this tug-of-war game. But just watch what happens if they yank their rope too hard against a wily opponent!

WHAT YOU NEED

- 2 stumps (4 to 10 inches tall) or milk crates
- 30 feet of rope
- 2 players

Set up the stumps or upside-down milk crates about 6 to 12 feet apart. Lay the rope between the platforms, leaving the surplus rope coiled at both ends. Standing on the platforms, the players pull or relax the rope, trying to get their opponent to lose his or her balance and step off. Might is not always right here, as a hard tug can be neutralized by a loosened grip — and the sudden slack can make the tugger teeter. Make sure to play this on a soft surface in case someone takes a tumble.

Hopscotch Game 2

The Sheridan family of Williamsville, New York, customized their yard with a personalized patio-stone hopscotch. They sanded ten patio stones, painted them white, numbered them, and then decorated each one with handprints and personal symbols. That meant an Elmo stamp for Kevin, a frog for amphibian-loving Michael. For Courtney, a serious hoop-shooter? A basketball, of course! They finished the stones with a coat of clear acrylic sealant and were ready to play.

A Crowd-squeezer

88 Here's a family game you can count on in a crunch. Spread a blanket on the grass and challenge everyone to pile on top so that no part of anyone's body touches the ground beyond the blanket. If the group succeeds, fold the blanket in half and try again. Continue in this way to see how small a space you all can fit on.

The Great Anything Hunt

89 Put those collecting skills to use with a colorful treasure hunt that can be played again and again.

WHAT YOU NEED

- Pebbles, acorns, or other treasures — at least 42; more if you've got a crowd
- Nontoxic acrylic paints in 6 colors (we used gold, red, green, purple, blue, and white)
- Paintbrushes

For the treasure, use whatever's plentiful around your backyard — rocks, shells, pieces of wood, and so on. Begin with some gathering: have your kids collect at least 42 pebbles, acorns, or other such objects. Spread out the objects on a sheet of newspaper and paint them as follows: two golds, four reds, six greens, eight purples, ten blues, and 12 whites (or use the colors of your choice). Each color carries a different point value: 10 points for gold, 8 for red, 6 for green, 4 for purple, 2 for blue, and 1 for white.

When the treasures are dry, one child or a grown-up can hide them around the yard. Then the hunt is on. Whoever amasses the most points is anointed Treasure Hunter Extraordinaire — at least until the next hunt begins.

Lame Hen

90 This relay race from China is great for parties. If you have only a few kids, try a beat-the-clock version. First, gather 20 straight sticks, about 2 feet long. Line up ten of them, each about 18 inches apart, like ladder rungs. A few feet away, do the same with the other ten sticks, making sure each line begins and ends in the same place. Teams line up about 15 feet behind the first stick. At the "Go" signal, the first player on each team hops on one foot over each stick, all the while squawking like a lame hen (little kids can bunny-hop on two feet). At the end of the row, the hen picks up the last stick, hops with it back to the starting line, and places it so that it is first in line. Then the next player starts hopping the course. The first team to get all its players through the course wins.

FUN FACT In 1992, Jerdone Coleman-McGhee of Texas won a place in *The Guinness Book of World Records* for stone-skipping: a record-breaking 38 skips!

Crab Soccer

91 Ten minutes of this game will leave kids bright-eyed and asking for more — and adults so spent they feel almost, um, soft-shelled.

WHAT YOU NEED

2 heavy-ply trash bags

Newspaper

Twist tie

Cloth tape

2 to 10 players

Make a crab soccer ball: double up the trash bags, stuff them with balled newspaper, twist-tie them closed, and tape the whole thing crosswise.

The game is played just like soccer, with the big exception that players can only run (make that scuttle) and kick in the crab position — in other words, in a sort of leaning-back, race-car-driver stance, with derriere just off the ground. Simply pick teams, set up two goals (marked by hats, old sneakers, and the like), gather for a kickoff, and you're in for major fun.

Summer Scavengers

"A few years ago, our family of five decided to spend our summer vacation at home. After enjoying day-trips to nearby cities, we came up with the idea of having our own Summer Scavenger Hunt. Everyone got to help choose the items on the list, which included a cookie from a local bakeshop, a brochure on Hawaii, fishing lures, a yard of material to make into an outfit for the baby, and the receipt for the smallest purchase. We had such a great time that we decided to make this hunt an annual event!" — Dawn Segura, Mesquite, Texas

A Cheesy Caper

92 In this fun whodunit, one child plays the part of the mouse, and the others are cheese bandits. The mouse places a yellow object (like a bottle cap or a bandanna) on the ground, then stands in front of it with her back to the group. While she silently counts to 20, one of the bandits sneaks up, snatches the object, and then attempts to hide it up his sleeve or somewhere else on his person. The mouse turns around and has one chance to guess which bandit scoffed the cheese. If she is correct, she gets a second round at being the mouse. If not, the kid who has the cheese gets a turn.

Blacktop Games

Coin Trick

93 Flipping a coin may not sound like much of a challenge to most kids, but in this contest, it's literally a long shot.

WHAT YOU NEED

Penny

Tennis ball

2 players

To start the game, two kids stand facing each other about 10 feet apart on a sidewalk. Place a penny on the ground between them. The first player then bounces a tennis ball to his opponent, attempting to hit the coin in the process. If he succeeds, he earns a point; if he flips the coin over, he scores 2 points. Next, the opponent tries his luck. The kids alternate turns. The first one to tally 21 points wins.

Turtle Race

94 Who's the one in your family who sticks out her neck a bit too far? You'll find out when you spend some time at the turtle races. To play, gather a sheet of lined paper (legal size works great) and a quarter and a penny for every player, plus two more coins to toss as dice. Mark a start line at the bottom of the paper and a finish line at the top. Each player gets a turtle — a quarter for the body and a penny for the head. Line up all the turtles with their heads at the starting line. Players take turns tossing the dice coins and moving their turtles as follows: two heads and you move your turtle's head two lines forward (and get to roll again); one head and one tail, and you move one line (and can toss again); two tails, and your turn is over — and you must slide your turtle's head back to its body, losing any headway you may have made during that turn. At any point before rolling two tails, a player can choose to end her turn by moving the body of her turtle forward to meet its head. Continue until one speedy turtle crosses the finish line.

Jump the Trap

95 This has to be the simplest game ever invented — and one of the most fiendishly difficult to get really good at. It's fast-paced, easy to play, and requires kids to do one of their favorite things: jump!

WHAT YOU NEED

Sturdy rope, 5 to 8 feet long

Shoe

3 to 8 players

Tie somebody's shoe to the end of the rope. (Kids have also been known to use a particularly detested textbook in place of the shoe. Social studies works well.) One player holds the shoeless end of the rope and spins around — not too fast — so that the rope sweeps in a circle. The weight keeps the rope fairly near the ground. Players must jump over the rope as it passes them (this is easiest if kids spread themselves around the circle so they're not all in one clump). If the shoe hits a player's foot or leg, he's out. The last person still jumping gets to turn the rope during the next round.

Little-kid variation: Don't make it an elimination game — just have everyone take turns jumping and spinning. Also, using a repetitive jump-rope rhyme can make it easier for kids to get a feel for the duration of each turn of the rope.

Skip It

96 Rope your kids into our jumping games.

Rhyme of Your Own: Tally how many times you can jump without missing by making up a rhyming jingle that ends in a count-off (such as "Candy, candy in the dish. How many pieces do you wish? One, two, three, four …").

Bag of Tricks: Players turning the rope (the enders) call out tasks to the jumpers, such as "touch the ground" or "take a bow." Whoever misses must relieve an ender, who gets a turn in the middle as a jumper.

Through the Windmill: Players line up on one side of the rope. One after another, each person jumps in, skips once, then jumps out and runs to the end of the line. Anyone who misses is out. With each round, the rope is turned faster to increase the challenge.

Switcheroo

98 Everybody wins in this fun group challenge that may remind you of that sixties party classic — Twister!

MATERIALS

Chalk

4 to 10 players

To play, use chalk to draw a row of connected boxes on a sidewalk. You'll need one more box than there are players. Then form two teams and have the players stand in the boxes with the empty box separating the two groups.

Explain that the object of the game is for both groups to successfully swap places while staying in the boxes. Now cue the players to start switching positions by moving into the unoccupied squares — a feat that may require stepping around one or more people. The only rule: just one person can occupy each box at any given time.

TRAINING GAME

Blading

97 Using any sort of cone (sand-filled plastic soda bottles or milk jugs), invent courses to skate through. For an extra challenge, pretend your course is an art museum and the cones are priceless vases.

NEW CLASSIC

Bike Rodeo

99 All you're gonna need for this kind of bronco bustin' is a standard-issue kid's bike. Just remember to trade in your ten-gallon hat for a sturdy helmet and to wait for the judge to call riders out one at a time.

Calf Roping: Each rider follows a chalked course, pausing at one point to set his or her feet on the ground, pick up a hula hoop, and toss it over a stool or other target before continuing to the finish line. Fastest time wins.

Barrel Racing: Riders maneuver bikes, in a clover-leaf pattern, around three cones. Give points for how close the riders come to the cones without knocking them over and how many loops they can make in a set amount of time.

Bronco Saddling: In a real rodeo, riders have to stay on a bronco for 8 seconds. To make this a bike event, draw a chalked circular course of tight turns and, if possible, hills and valleys. Time each contestant. The champion is the rider who follows the course and keeps his feet on the pedals the longest without touching the ground.

Sidewalk Creatures

100 Drawing these friendly monsters will bring out the Dr. Frankenstein lurking inside even the most mild-mannered child.

WHAT YOU NEED

Paper and pencil

Tape

Large bucket of sidewalk chalk
 (at least a dozen pieces)

Begin by cutting the paper into small strips, then label each strip with the name of a particular body part: car, cyc, nose, feet, hair, and so on — everything but the head. Don't forget to include monster essentials like horns and claws. Tape one label around each piece of chalk and put all the pieces in a bucket. A parent can start the game by drawing an oval (or the shape of your choice) for the head. Then each artist dips into the chalk bucket and adds to the creature whatever the label directs. Allow plenty of room for creativity, and don't be bound by naturalistic constraints — six eyes or three legs are perfectly acceptable.

Chalk Walk

101 Equipped with nothing more than a box of chalk, your kids can turn the walkway that leads to your front door into a trail of adventure for a parent or special visitors. (Don't forget to tip off guests before they arrive so they'll be prepared to play along.) For inspiration, you may want to suggest to the young designers a few imaginary obstacles, such as:

◆ **A narrow, winding road with a dramatic hairpin curve**

◆ **A scary or enchanted forest with a pine tree maze**

◆ **A lake or raging river (include stepping-stones or a rickety bridge for crossing)**

Mock Chalk

102 This tough version is ideal for sidewalk use. Mix 2 parts plaster of Paris with 1 part warm water and add powdered tempera paint to get the desired color. For each stick, line a toilet paper tube with waxed paper, seal one end with tape, and pour in the mixture. Tap the tube to release bubbles. Let harden.

CHAPTER FOUR

Rainy-day Play

Absorbing activities to keep your family's disposition sunny —

even when the weather isn't

W HEN IT COMES to kids, water seemingly has the power to both attract and repel. Give kids a snorkel mask, and they'll spend the entire day underwater. They'll dive into pools, jump through waves, race through sprinklers, and splash in the tub until their fingers look like raisins. But natural precipitation — especially the kind that lasts for days, or weeks, on end — is rarely met with such exuberance. When we wake up every morning to rain, rain, and more rain, we start to feel a simmering hostility toward the weather. And with a houseful of bored kids, a few rainy days can take on the proportions of a monsoon.

What's a sodden family to do? Plenty. As certain as the flowers grow after a shower, our kids' creativity actually blooms in a storm. Long afternoons beg to be filled with games — the old favorites and maybe some new ones. Kids and parents curl up with good books. Imaginations hum: a box

begins to look like a spaceship, or maybe even a grocery store.

On the following pages, you'll find some of our favorite indoor activities to do during downpours (or during a snowstorm or even a heat wave). We've avoided the obvious suggestions (presumably you've already thought of puzzles and Monopoly) in favor of alternatives, like the Pet Vet on page 79, that have worked for our families on the grayest of indoor days. With a minimum of preparation and the following tips, you and your kids will be happy to let it rain on your parade.

Jump-start an activity.

House-bound kids may be quick to cry boredom, but they are equally quick to become engrossed. More often than not, a few minutes of planning, preparing, and playing an activity with our kids is all they require from us, and then they're off and running on their own. Teach them the rules to crazy eights, play a few hands yourself, then leave them to their own card tournament. Dig out the tape recorder

Fabulous Finger Puppets, page 72

and interview your kids; then they can spend the next hour perfecting the weather report — a bucket of fun, even if the news is bad.

Plan a surprise project. Do something that surprises your children, and they'll be talking about it for many a gray day to come. At lunchtime, try a change of scenery and set out an indoor picnic on the living room floor. Or fill the tub with bubbles and pool toys, invite your kids to an indoor pool party (dressed in their bathing suits, of course), and watch them soak the blues away.

Bring the outdoors in. Shake things up by suggesting that the kids play some classic outdoor games inside, such as marbles or blowing bubbles. If you have a playroom, you might also let the kids set up a campsite with a blanket tent and flashlights. One *FamilyFun* contributor moved in her Little Tikes slide one long winter so her kids could get some exercise.

Sing in the rain. In the spirit of, If you can't lick 'em, join 'em, we offer this pleasurable last resort. Make sure your kids are dressed for the weather (say, rain jackets and rubber boots in the spring, or swimsuits and flip-flops in the summer) and send them out. Half the pleasure will be the breach of custom; the other half will be mud and sogginess. Let them kick around in puddles, or try our Watercolor Chalk Painting (page 95). They can even decorate an umbrella for the occasion (page 92).

Rainy-day Classics

* Bake a batch of chocolate-chip cookies
* Write and read secret codes
* Make a big bowl of popcorn and watch a favorite video
* Hide pennies throughout the house and have the kids find them
* Build a card house
* Have a round-robin thumb-wrestling contest
* Make a paper doll chain
* Build a sofa-cushion fort
* Have a gin rummy tournament
* Fold paper airplanes and launch them in the living room

Puppets

Tiny Dancers

103 Your child will stay on her toes with this pirouetting troupe of finger-puppet ballerinas. Plus, she can use them to act out her favorite poem or fairy tale.

MATERIALS

- Poster board and construction paper
- Colored markers and glue
- Googly eyes (optional)
- 18- by 13-inch strip of Bubble Wrap
- 1 pipe cleaner
- Fingernail polish

To make a paper dancer, sketch a simple ballerina silhouette on the poster board. Draw the head, torso, and arms held upright (called *en couronne*, "like a crown") but do not include the legs. Cut out the sketch and draw on a hairdo, facial features, and a leotard with colored markers. Or you can glue on construction paper hair and clothes, as well as googly eyes. Near the lower edge of the torso, cut out a pair of legholes that your child can comfortably fit her fingers through.

For a frilly tutu, thread a pipe cleaner through one long edge of the Bubble Wrap, gathering it as you go. Then wrap the tutu around the ballerina's waist and twist together the pipe cleaner ends behind her back. Finally, your child can turn her fingernails into a pair of ballet slippers by brushing on a coat of satiny polish.

A Show of Hands

104 When it comes to entertaining kids, these stagehands are right for the job.

To create one, have your child hold his hand in a loose fist with the end of his thumb tucked into the center, as shown at right. Next, he should practice wiggling the lower portion of his thumb to simulate a talking mouth. Now create the puppet: using different shades of lipstick or face paints, draw on lips and eyes. Add eyelashes and other details with an eyeliner pencil. Finally, tape on a bunched yarn wig or a felt cone hat.

It's Showtime!

105 Pick up a roll of tickets at an office supply store – they cost just a few dollars – and use them to jump-start pretend play. Kids can collect the tickets from the audience (parents, siblings, and neighbors) for a puppet show, an at-home movie night, or an impromptu dance performance. To round out the show, set up chairs for the audience and serve refreshments (popcorn!) during intermission. Enjoy the show!

106 Fabulous Finger Puppets

Lights! Fingers! Action! Make our finger puppets and let the show begin.

Flutter Bye

Cut off a finger from an old glove for an easy start to our cheery butterfly. Then cut out a set of cardboard wings and affix dot stickers in a contrasting color. Hot-glue or staple pipe cleaner antennae onto the top center of the wings and glue on the glove finger body. Draw on a simple face — less is more for this kid-pleasing favorite.

The Not-so-scary Dragon

Don't be fooled by the fire breath — this guy is a softy. Start with a glove finger and glue on two small buttons for eyes. Cut a set of spiky scales from a piece of felt and glue on. Make a mouth from green cardboard lined with orange paper and staple tissue paper flames inside. Bend the mouth to shape it and glue it on.

Princess Pinky

Start with a tongue-depressor base. Wrap the stick in a bright fabric scrap, then secure it in place with glue and a band of decorative ribbon. Braid lengths of yarn at both ends, tie with glittery pipe cleaners, and glue in place. Top with a crown of cardboard and sequins. Lastly, draw on a sweet face with markers. Variations: Use a larger set of clothes to create a truly noble queen, or, with darker colors and fancier trim, an evil queen.

Big-mouth Bird

For our comical squawking bird, start with a brightly colored glove finger. Glue on two buttons for eyes. Add a cardboard mouth folded into shape with an open beak. Pierce three colorful feathers — they don't even need to match — through the glove-finger base. Add a dab of glue inside and out to hold them in place.

Good King Thumbkin

Wrap a tongue depressor in a royal shade of felt, leaving an inch or two exposed at the top. Over that, wrap a contrasting piece of felt for a dashing cape, and for a truly royal look, glue on trim of braid or lace. Use a bit of cotton ball for a beard (on the front) and hair (on the back). Glue on a paper crown and draw on a face, haughty or wise, depending on your political view of this particular royal family. **Variation:** A smaller suit of clothes, with yarn hair in a bowl cut, should produce a fairly charming prince.

Zoomy Rocket Ship

This easy rider starts with a base of cardboard on a tongue depressor, which is covered with construction paper and decorated with markers. Glue on tissue paper for rocket flames. Or make a car, with tissue paper exhaust. The car wheels can be part of a one-piece shape or cut out separately and glued onto the car. An important detail: build transportation only after you've got a few puppets ready. That way, you can make your vehicles with the finished puppets in mind — you want to be sure the windows are big enough for the puppets' heads to fit through, so it looks like they're really going for a ride.

A Classic Tale

The key to a great puppet show is having just enough script to know what to do next, but not so much that there's no place for hilarious ad-libbing. The following plot should inspire your kids to develop more stories on their own.

The Dream Team

An evil king rules the land, and the puppets must band together to overthrow him. In the process, each discovers he has a special talent: the bird can fly and do reconnaissance; perhaps the dragon can become invisible (simply by ducking down out of the stage!); and so on. Work out the basic order of things ahead of time, as well as the final scene, in which the king is either tricked into leaving the castle and then surrounded, or tricked into giving up his crown, and thus the throne. Let each kid decide his characters' special powers. At the end, the evil king may be reformed or led away in shame to an ignominious fate as a castle servant.

FUN IN A BOX

Set the Stage

107 A sturdy box and tension curtain rods transform a doorway into a theater. When the show's over, it doubles as an under-bed storage corral for all the puppets.

MATERIALS

- Sturdy cardboard box, 2 feet wide
- Craft knife
- Straightedge
- Packing tape
- 3 tension curtain rods
- Construction paper, crayons, and markers
- Old curtain

1. With a craft knife (a parent's job), carefully trim the sides of the box to 7 or so inches high.

2. Cut a trapezoidal notch in one of the longer sides, as shown at right, top, to give the puppeteers more room to work.

3. With a straightedge, draw a rectangle in the middle of the box's bottom for the stage opening, then cut it out (you'll probably have to cut through two layers of flaps). With packing tape, secure the loose edges of the flaps and reinforce any weak seams.

4. Cut four holes for two of the tension rods. Each hole should be centered in the sidewall and as close to the seam as possible.

5. Now it's time to decorate. We covered the box with construction paper, then decorated it with crayons and markers.

6. Finally, thread the curtain on the third tension rod and hang it in the doorway just below the stage. The curtain will give your puppeteers the privacy to work their dramatic magic.

Pretend Play

Stocking the Store

Open up shop with the following items:

- Tape empty boxes closed; try cereal (minis are fun), pasta, crackers, even tissue boxes

- Fill clean, empty plastic bottles with beans or colored water

- Duct-tape the sharp edges of clean, empty soup, veggie, fruit, or tuna cans (or donate a few full cans to the cause)

- Make fake food out of self-hardening clay

- Add price tags, stock up on paper bags, and get ready for business

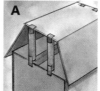

FUN IN A BOX

Open a Corner Market

108 With some clever renovations, an empty refrigerator box becomes a store full of fun.

MATERIALS

- **Refrigerator box, approximately 30 by 32 by 64 inches**
- **Packing and masking tapes**
- **Utility knife**
- **Yardstick and pencil**
- **Extra cardboard and boxes**
- **Paper towel tubes**
- **Paint roller (optional)**
- **Acrylic paints and paintbrushes**
- **Twine**

Seal the refrigerator box top and bottom with packing tape. Using the utility knife (a parent's job), cut a window in the box's front and a door in one side.

To make the sloped roof, cut a 30- by 45-inch piece of cardboard and score it into thirds, as shown in Figure A, above. Cut four 8-inch lengths of paper towel tube for roof supports. Use masking tape to attach two supports to each side edge of the roof. Lay the cardboard over the supports, as shown, and tape in place.

Now it's time to decorate. Your kids can use a paint roller to apply large areas of paint to the box or use paintbrushes for more detailed work, such as stripes, trim, flowers, or signs.

To make the fruit bin, cut the flaps off an approximately 10- by 23- by 5-inch box. Poke two holes in the rear corners of the small box, as shown in Figure B, and two holes just under each corner of the store's front window. From inside the store, thread a short piece of twine out through the wall, through both holes in the bin, and back through the wall, then knot both ends of the twine. Repeat for the other end of the bin. Use this same technique to make bins or shelves inside the store. For a mailbox or cash drawer, tape a cereal or cracker box to the wall.

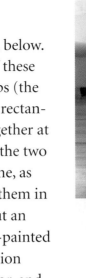

Doggy Digs

109 If your child has a stuffed animal that would love a place of its very own, here's just the thing — a cozy cardboard abode that's fun and easy to construct.

MATERIALS

- Cardboard box, about 12 inches square
- Utility knife
- Masking or packing tape
- Paint, sponges, and construction paper

Open the top flaps of the box and cut one quarter of the way down each corner, as shown in Figure A, below. Starting from the bottoms of these cuts, fold in two opposite flaps (the longer flaps, if you're using a rectangular box) and tape them together at the top to form a peak. Trim the two side flaps to match the roofline, as shown in Figure B, and tape them in place against the roof. Cut out an arched doorway, add sponge-painted roof shingles and a construction paper nameplate over the door, and your house is ready for its first tenant.

A

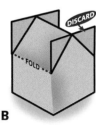

B

Shoe Store

111 Got time to fill? This soleful shop is a shoe-in. Have your child gather a row of shoes before asking customers to step right up – onto a ruler, so she can measure their feet. Let her fit a few pairs on game shoppers (set up a mirror on the floor for ogling them), then wrap the chosen shoes in tissue paper, put them in a box, and ring up the sale on a toy cash register.

Build a Skyscraper

110 A big case of boredom sometimes requires a big cure — like this towering, build-it-yourself skyscraper. Start by collecting cardboard boxes in various sizes. Tape the boxes shut with packing tape, then stack and tape them atop each other. Using markers or crayons, your kids can decorate the boxes with windows, columns, gargoyles, and mailboxes. They might add some 3-D touches such as tissue paper flowers and bushes or paper flags. **Crafter's Tip:** If you don't have plain brown boxes, wrap yours with butcher paper or turn them inside out and tape them back together.

Indoor Explorer

"One winter day, my three-year-old daughter, Kara, wanted to go hiking — a great idea, except for subzero weather. So I found a cowboy hat, my wife's vest, a shoulder purse, a toy camera, and Kara's hiking boots, and dressed her up to look like an explorer. I made her wait in the family room while I hid her stuffed animals around the house. I told her that her job was to shoot pictures of each of the animals she found. The expedition was a hit!"

— Steve Argue, Wauwatosa, Wisconsin

Ride a Hobbyhorse

112 Fashioned from a pair of old blue jeans, this steed requires no sewing.

MATERIALS

- **Pair of old blue jeans**
- **String, glue, and felt**
- **140 eight-inch lengths of black yarn**
- **Polyester filling**
- **3-foot-long, ¾-inch dowel**

Cut off one jean leg about 2 feet up from the hem. Turn the leg inside out and tie it closed with string. Now turn the leg right side out and glue on felt eyes and nostrils. For the mane and forelock, arrange the yarn into four equal bunches. Tie each bunch in the center with another strand. Starting 2 inches above the horse's eyes in the center of the pant leg, cut eight ¾-inch vertical slits (spaced ½ inch apart). Weave one bunch of yarn though the first two slits so that the ends stick out and resemble a forelock. Weave the other bunches through the remaining slits to create the mane.

For ears, cut the back pockets from the jeans and tie the tops closed with string. Cut ear slits in the head and insert the tied ends of the pockets into them. Stuff the horse's head (up to its ears) with polyester filling. Insert one end of the dowel. Pack the neck with more filling and tightly tie the lower edge of the neck to the dowel. Finally, tie a string bridle around the horse's nose.

Box Car Derby

113 Cut from empty cereal boxes, this freeway will be open to traffic in no time. To cut sections of straight track from each box, draw a line all the way around the box ½ inch up from the bottom. Cut along the line, then snip away the walls on the ends. In the same manner, cut additional pieces from the sides of the box. Use the remaining scraps to cut out corners and guardrails (for a curve, staple two pieces of track to a flat pie-slice shape and staple on a narrow guardrail). Create an overpass by cutting an archway into a tea box, or use a few boxes to build a gas station. Finally, tape the track together any way you like.

Open a Doll Spa

115 When the weather is frightful, help your child warm up the afternoon with a play sauna for her dolls. Fill a basin, baby tub, or even your bathroom tub with warm

water, cover the bathroom floor with towels (so you just won't care what happens), and let your kids bathe their dolls and all their tiny clothes. Use a mild shampoo, and set up a drying rack with clothespins. Have on hand a few beauty products for after the bath: hooded towels, combs, hair ribbons, and talcum powder. A toy car wash for miniature cars can be equally fun, especially if you have a handheld shower nozzle. Afterward, organize the sparkling fleet for a car show.

Pretend Party

114 Barbie's big day? Surprise your child and her play date with a make-believe birthday party for their favorite doll. Round up a festive assortment of supplies: balloons, hats, and streamers create an instant party atmosphere. You can get a bit more elaborate with goody bags (just fill paper bags with saved favors from past parties), gala table settings, and iced muffins or cupcakes (add candles!). Or add a present for the birthday girl — maybe that rodeo outfit Barbie's been eyeing, nicely wrapped and ribboned (she might need a little help unwrapping it, of course).

Bath Craft

116 This clever catamaran turns your bathtub into a glamorous port of call. To make one, remove the labels from two plastic soda bottles. Clamp the bottles together temporarily with rubber bands, then wrap them with colored tape, as shown below. Remove the rubber bands, then, with a craft knife (a parent's job), cut the oval seat openings. Sail away with a crew of fashion dolls, action figures, or waterproof plush toys.

Fort, Inc.

117 If your kids are in the business of serious play, take a memo: our easy blanket fort makes the perfect corporate hideaway for young tyke-oons.

MATERIALS

Sheet or blanket, card table, and couch pillows

Cardboard, scissors, markers, and junk mail

Briefcase, telephone, computer keyboard, and in/out boxes

Office supplies (see the Junior Executive Kit on page 23)

To make office space, your child can drape a sheet or blanket over the table and prop up a few pillows for a peaked roof. Now she can stock the office with various supplies — whatever she needs for pretend scenarios (these might include conference calls, meetings, memos, or briefings). Tape up a mail slot cut from cardboard and labeled with markers. Once or twice a day, a postal worker should drop through a new load of junk mail (finally, a good use for it!), and office workers can sort it into in/out boxes or file folders.

Indoor Camp-out

118 Answer the call of the wild with a retreat to the great indoors. Your child can set up a basic table-cushion-sheet tent (see the fort above), grab a canteen, and unfurl some sleeping bags. Other props can enhance the encamped effect: marshmallows are a must, as is a flashlight, and your camper will doubtless require a compass to locate provisions fridgeward. Finally, a book of scary stories might sound the right note, and a strategically placed teddy bear can growl around outside the tent (cuddling will likely tame the beast).

Chair Choo-choo

119 All aboard! Please take your seats (or is that *chairs*?). When stir-crazy kids are craving a little loco-motion, a make-believe train might be just the ticket. Simply set the dining room chairs in a straight line (or two by two), and the kids can pretend they're aboard the *Orient-Express* — or a jumbo jet, a horse-drawn carriage, even a roller coaster. Props might include conductors' hats, suitcases, and paper tickets with a hole punch. Destinations are limitless: the kids can chug toward Grandma's house or take the zoo-bound express, fly over their hometown ("Hey, is that our school down there?") or visit distant imaginary places (Narnia, Hogwarts, Neverland). If the trip turns out to be a long one, a designated attendant (hint, hint) can come around with juice and pretzels on a tray.

Tiny Tollbooth

121 Rev up toy car play with an easy pasta-box tollbooth. Simply remove the transparent window from the box, then add a gate (we attached a strip of cardboard with a paper fastener) and an action-figure toll-taker. Pennies, please!

Pet Vet

120 Got a feverish Beanie Baby? A dancing bear with a sprained ankle? Emergency Pet Vet to the rescue! Kids love to feel useful, even if it's just pretend, and the drama of nursing ill stuffies can occupy them happily for hours.

MATERIALS

- Play doctor's kit
- Tray
- Large craft sticks, gauze, tape, and empty pill bottles
- Dish towel, 2 wrapping paper tubes, and tape

A play doctor's kit can be easily adapted to fuzzy patients (stethoscopes and syringes are a must). Round out the supply tray with craft sticks (perfect for splints), gauze, tape, and pill bottles. Make a pet rescue stretcher by slinging the dish towel between the wrapping paper tubes and taping it in place. Some vigorous brushing, a snack, and a few tender kisses will cure even an animal who resists all other treatment.

Rainy-day Play

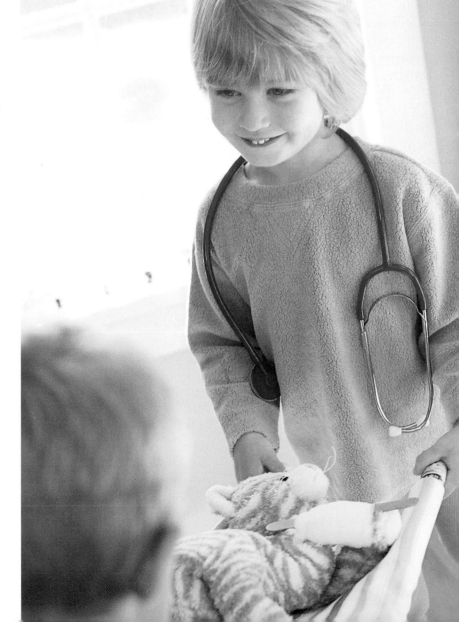

Dress Up

Pack a Costume Suitcase

122 To encourage hours of magic, masquerade, and make-believe, pack old suitcases with dress-ups and disguises and store them under your child's bed. We recommend scouring your closets, attic, and local thrift store for the following:

- ◆ Fancy old dresses, scarves, and purses
- ◆ Hats — top, straw, witch, and cowboy hats; fedoras; Easter bonnets; baseball caps; chef's toques
- ◆ A feather boa
- ◆ A piece of sheer, velvet, or heavy fabric with a dress clip — an instant cape!
- ◆ Shoes of all kinds — cowboy boots, feathered mules, Chinese slippers, high heels
- ◆ A bathrobe or kimono
- ◆ Wigs and fake fur for beards and sideburns
- ◆ A bandanna
- ◆ Costume jewelry, including bangle bracelets and clip-on earrings
- ◆ Eyeware — think nonprescription glasses, shades, and swim goggles
- ◆ Lipstick
- ◆ A black eye pencil (and cold cream) for whiskers and mustaches
- ◆ Plastic fangs
- ◆ Wands
- ◆ A tiara
- ◆ Angel wings
- ◆ A tutu
- ◆ Masks
- ◆ Old neckties
- ◆ Silk flowers

Clothes Quarters

"My daughters, Chandler and Kelsey, just love to play dress-up. The sight of their clothes all wrinkled up in a box drove me crazy, so we made each of the girls a portable closet from cardboard boxes. We cut openings for the clothes and shoes, added bars for hanging, and covered the boxes with Con-Tact paper. Now the girls each have a wardrobe fit for a princess."

— Robin Giese, Trappe, Pennsylvania

I Want to Be a ...

Doctor: Grab a white jacket (pop some tongue depressors in the pocket), a stethoscope, a disposable dust mask (for surgical rounds), a bottle of jelly bean pills, and a pair of glasses.

Superhero: Don a cape (a towel and a safety pin will do in a pinch), an eye mask, a felt *S* to pin to your T-shirt, and a pair of blue tights or long underwear.

Princess: Drape yourself in everything fancy (including anything velvet or satin or rhinestone), pin on lots of ribbons and lace, thread gold cord through your hair, and don't forget a tiara!

Deep-sea Diver: Slip into your swimsuit, add fins and a snorkel mask, and hop in the tub.

Positively Presley

123 The King is reputed to have spent more than $15,000 a month on his wardrobe, but your kids can impersonate him for a song. To orchestrate your own Elvis tribute, cut out two long sideburns from fake fur (sold at fabric stores) and snip a pair of small holes near the top of each one. Thread the sideburns onto the stems of a pair of gold-trimmed Elvis-style sunglasses, and it's showtime.

COSTUME PROP

Terrific Tiaras

124 Little princesses will love decorating their own crowns. Cut a basic tiara shape from metallic silver poster board. Trim the midsection to create a fancy edge. Your child can adorn her crown with stickers and plastic gems (sold at most craft stores) attached with double-sided tape. To fit each crown, wrap it around the princess's head and paper-clip the overlapped ends.

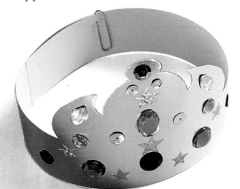

COSTUME PROP

Magic Wands

125 What's a wizard without his wand? No need to find out. Use a craft knife (a parent's job) to cut a foot of ½-inch clear, inflexible plastic aquarium tubing (sold in pet stores). Seal one end of the tube with a bit of modeling clay. Then your child can fill his tube with wiggle worms (metallic pipe cleaners) and dragon scales (sequins or glitter) before sealing the other end with clay.

QUICK DISGUISE

Five-minute Masks

126 Here are easy ways to go incognito using household items.

Mask 1: Tape a poster-board face with nose- and eyeholes inside the front edge of a winter hat. Add paper or yarn hair around the sides of the hat.

Mask 2: Start with a medium-size paper bag (to be worn upside down over your head). Shape it by cutting the sides and back into hair. Cut facial features into the front, and round the bottom into a chin.

Mask 3: Make an animal nose from an egg-carton cup by poking airholes in it and attaching string ties. Decorate by attaching pipe cleaner cat whiskers, a cardboard bird beak, etcetera.

Indoor Games

Play Cards

127 On a rainy day, let a deck of cards be your ace in the hole.

Gather some potato-chip poker chips and remind your kids of these old favorites.

Ages 4 to 6: concentration, slapjack, go fish

Ages 6 to 8: war, pig, old maid, crazy eights

Ages 8 to 10: I doubt it, spoons, casino, spit, hearts

Ages 10 and up: Michigan, rummy 500, cribbage, spite and malice

Pick a Card

128 This trick takes some practice – and a pinch of salt. Have a friend shuffle the deck and pick a card. Have another friend cut the deck into two piles. Ask the cardholder to look at his card. As he does, grab a pinch of salt (it's in your pocket). Tell him to put the card facedown on one of the piles. As you point to which pile, slyly sprinkle on a little salt. After he places his card down, put the other pile back on top. Tap the side of the deck (it should separate at the salt). Hold up the top portion: there's your friend's card.

Kentucky Card Derby

129 Here's how your family can stage some racing excitement on your own turf with a simple card game that can be just as unpredictable as the derby itself.

To get things off and running, have each player choose a suit. Take the corresponding jacks (jockeys, if you will) from the deck and place them side by side face-up on a tabletop. Shuffle the rest of the deck and set it facedown beside the jacks.

Now take turns flipping over the card at the top of the deck. If the card matches a player's suit, he gets to lay the card faceup end to end with his jack; if not, it goes into the discard pile. Continue in this manner until all of the cards have been used or discarded. The person with the longest track of cards wins.

"Do you start building from the top or the bottom?"

— The all-time favorite question asked of Bryan Berg, holder of the world record for the largest card house: a 127-story tower measuring 24 feet 4 inches, built in 1999

Game Night

"As a welcome change from TV, we invite the kids in our neighborhood over for game nights. We have a different theme each time — board games, for example — and a themed treat (such as puzzle-piece-shaped cookies on Puzzle Night). The kids learn new skills (making conversation, taking turns, and winning and losing gracefully), and they have fun!"

—Margaret Connor, Austin, Texas

Marble Maze

131

To get the good times rolling on a rainy afternoon, make one of these amazing cardboard towers.

MATERIALS

- **7 wrapping paper or mailing tubes**
- **Pencil and ruler**
- **Craft knife**
- **2 small plastic margarine tubs**
- **Uncooked rice**
- **Marbles**

Construct the tower posts. Start with the left one. Set a tube on end. Draw a pencil line from top to bottom, then mark five points along it 2, 8, 10, 19, and 21 inches from the top. With a craft knife (adults only), cut a hole around each mark that's just big enough to accommodate the end of another tube. For the right post, position the holes 4, 6, 13, 15, and 25 inches from the top, then cut one more hole (where the marble will exit the maze) in the opposite side of the tube 25¾ inches from the top.

Anchor the posts. Make a base for each post by cutting a hole in the bottom of a margarine tub. Put the lid on the tub, then set the tub upside down on the floor and pour the rice into the hole, filling the tub.

Make tunnels. Next, transform four more tubes into crossings. Holding each one horizontally, cut a U-shaped opening in the upper wall at one end and in the lower wall at the opposite end. For the tower's lowest tunnel, cut a U-shaped opening in one end only of a fifth tube. Then cut peepholes in the tops of each tube.

Assemble the tower. Starting at the top of the tower, fit the tunnel ends into the post holes, as shown at left, so that the ends with openings in the upper wall are raised and the uncut end of the fifth tunnel extends to the exit hole. Finally, if your tower is a bit wobbly, you can stretch extralarge rubber bands or loop string around the posts for stability.

INSTANT GAME

Bowling Pin Derby

130

First make ten bowling pins. For each one, press a lump of clay into the bottom of a disposable plastic cup, invert a second cup over the first, and tape together the rims. To play, set up the pins in a triangular formation. Each player gets three consecutive rolls of a ball to knock down as many pins as possible. If all the pins fall before the third roll, reset them and continue. You get 1 point for each fallen pin. So if you're really lucky, you can get 30 points in one turn. The person with the most points after three rounds wins the game.

Penguin Games

132 When researchers first observed penguins hopping aboard ice floes and going for a ride, they weren't quite sure what it was about. Was it a territorial ritual, or a means of avoiding predators?

Ultimately, the scientists decided the birds were only having fun. Here's how your kids can have a penguin-style blast of their own playing a toastier indoor version of the game on a rainy (or arctic) afternoon.

Lay a trail of pillow ice floes about 2 feet apart on a cleared, carpeted floor. Have everyone line up single file (this is how penguins migrate north) and take turns hopping from pillow to pillow.

The penguins must land with both feet on each ice floe; if they don't, they are considered to have fallen in the drink and must step aside. Space the pillows farther apart for each new round until all but one penguin, the winner, has been eliminated.

Indoor Gardening

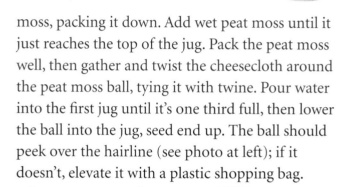

The Jug Heads

133 All it takes is water and sun to make these grassy-haired garden friends. Their jug heads make tidy, easy-to-water planters.

MATERIALS

- Pencil and permanent markers
- Two 1-gallon jugs
- Plastic milk caps and coffee-can or margarine-tub lids
- Foam mounting tape (available at craft stores)
- 1 square yard of cheesecloth
- Spray bottle and water
- Peat moss (about 3 quarts)
- Grass seed
- Twine
- Plastic margarine tub

To make a head, draw a hairline around one of the jugs, about two thirds up from the bottom. Cut away the top with scissors. Cut a nose and ears out of the excess plastic. To make the eyes, start with two milk caps. Then cut two white circles from a lid, making them just smaller than the caps. Using markers, draw an iris and pupil onto each circle, then attach the circles to the caps with foam tape. Cut a mouth from a plastic lid. Tape all the features to the jug.

To make a holder for the soil and seed bag, cut off the top of the second jug so that it's an inch taller than the first. Line the second jug with cheesecloth, letting it extend over the sides. Spray it lightly with water. Sprinkle a thin layer of peat moss over the cheesecloth, then cover the peat moss completely with grass seed.

In a mixing bowl, mix 6 cups of peat moss with 1 cup of water until the peat moss is moist. Cover the grass seed with a layer of wet peat moss, packing it down. Add wet peat moss until it just reaches the top of the jug. Pack the peat moss well, then gather and twist the cheesecloth around the peat moss ball, tying it with twine. Pour water into the first jug until it's one third full, then lower the ball into the jug, seed end up. The ball should peek over the hairline (see photo at left); if it doesn't, elevate it with a plastic shopping bag.

In a sunny spot, place the head on top of an overturned margarine tub neck. Spray with water and repeat twice a day until the grass sprouts.

Grow a Sweet Potato

134 The perfect indoor gardening project, this sweet-potato vine is quick and easy to grow.

MATERIALS

- Sweet potato that's begun to sprout
- 2 toothpicks
- Glass jar
- Terra-cotta pot and potting soil

Pierce the middle of the sweet potato with toothpicks, one on each side, and suspend it over the jar. Fill the jar almost to the top with lukewarm water and set it on a bright windowsill. Be sure that the root end of the potato, called the pointier, faces downward.

In seven to 14 days, you'll see whiskery rootlets growing under the water. In a week or two, you should see tiny red sprouts at the top, which will soon open into red-veined green leaves.

When growth is about 6 to 8 inches high, transplant the potato to a flowerpot. Fill the pot about a third of the way with soil, put in the tuber, and add soil up to the growth. Cover the tuber completely to discourage rotting. Water often to keep the soil lightly moist.

Tiny Terrarium

135 To grow a garden under glass, first head to your local garden center. Pick up a few plants (small ivies or palms) and small bags of stone, horticulture charcoal, and potting soil. At home, layer ½ inch of stone, ½ inch of charcoal, and 1½ inches of soil in a widemouthed jar. Plant the greenery, moisten the soil, and cap the jar. Keep in a well-lit place, but not in direct sunlight. If water beads up inside, uncap the jar and let it dry out. If beading doesn't reoccur, water the plants with a mister about once every two to four weeks.

Fancy Faux Flowerpots

136 Brighten a rainy day with a pot of beaded flowers. First, thread a green bead stem onto beading wire and knot the end. Next, add color beads for the flowers and knot the end.

To create petals, bend the flower-colored beads into an oval petal shape and twist the loop closed. Repeat these steps to create three or four more petals. When the petals are complete, wrap bare wire around the center of the flower to reduce the space between petals, then snip off the excess wire.

To plant each flower, press the wire into a mini flowerpot, filled with brown nonhardening modeling clay.

Carrots: Paint Brazil nuts orange, then glue on stems of artificial foliage.

Radishes: Paint hazelnuts white and red, then glue on green pipe cleaner stems.

Tools: Cut shovel and hoe blades from a foil pie plate. Glue onto trimmed bamboo skewers.

Scarecrow: Use tacky glue to secure two sticks (one with a V for the legs) and a walnut together. Wrap the figure with fabric strips for clothes. Glue on yarn hair and a straw hat from a craft store.

GARDEN CRAFT

Tabletop Garden

137 Not only does this tabletop garden make a whimsical decoration, but it's also a great project for young gardeners who are eager for sunny weather to come.

MATERIALS

Potting soil

Aluminum foil tray (11 by 16 inches)

Clear plastic bag or plastic wrap

Shade-mix grass seed

Craft sticks, glue, and white acrylic paint

To grow the grass for your mini yard, pour the potting soil into the foil tray and pat it down flat. Sprinkle on a layer of grass seed, then cover with a light layer of soil, pressing it down gently.

Water the soil, then loosely cover the tray (do not seal) with the clear plastic bag or plastic wrap. Check your garden regularly and remove the plastic when you see the first sprouts. Keep the soil lightly and evenly moist, and you should have a tray full of grass within three weeks. You may have to mow your grass!

To create the garden plot, use a butter knife to remove the grass from a small section of the tray and replace it with a layer of fresh potting soil. Now install a picket fence. To make each section, use scissors to trim the tops of seven craft sticks into points (a parent's job), then lay them in a row, equally spaced. Glue two uncut sticks across them. Once the glue has dried, turn over the sticks and glue two more across the back. When dry, paint the fence white. Set the fence sections in the soil and fill your garden with tiny vegetables, mini gardening tools, and a scarecrow (at right).

Music Time

Thimble Fingers

139 With these clever percussion gloves on, you'll feel like you have tap shoes on your fingertips.

All you need are ten metal thimbles, an old pair of gloves that fit your child's hands snugly, white glue, and ten pens. Simply stick the pens inside the gloves (one in each finger and thumb), glue the thimbles onto the top of each glove digit, let dry, remove the pens, and you're ready. Gloves like these are sometimes used by washboard players in zydeco music (creole dance music from Louisiana) to make sounds on a ribbed metal board. Try your tappers on tabletops, bathtub tiles, and any other surfaces that sound good to your ears.

INSTANT FUN

Spin a Marker Spiral

138 Have your kids ever seen anything so archaic as a record player? While you dig out your old one, have them choose a few washable markers. Poke a hole in the center of a paper plate, set it on the phonograph as you would a record, and turn on the player. Have your kids hold the tips of one or more markers on the plate, moving them back and forth. Flip over the plate and repeat on the other side. If you like, use scissors to cut around the spiral until you reach the plate's middle, then string up one end of the strip and let it hang down in a colorful curlicue.

Rainy-day Play

Music Box

140 If you want to foster impromptu jams and performances in your house, create a music box (or basket) and keep it handy. To fill it, start with some of the following instruments, and keep an eye out for used instruments at tag sales and in friends' attics: kazoo • triangle • shakers • finger cymbals • sticks • bells • drums • inexpensive guitar or ukulele • recorder • harmonica

INSTANT FUN
Dance to the Music!

On a gray day, when sunlight is scarce, try filling your house with another sensory pleasure, namely music. Put on some upbeat tunes and play **Do What I Do.** The leader performs a motion and everyone dances around the rug, doing it. Switch leaders with every song.

HOMEMADE INSTRUMENT
Bottled Music

141 Who hasn't blown across the lip of a half-empty pop bottle and marveled at the richness of the tone? As for what tone it was, however, that was anybody's guess. Well, no longer. In the box at right, we've calculated just how much water you need in eight 20-ounce pop bottles to create a major scale. Affix numbers to each bottle, 1 through 8 (or use different-colored stickers for younger kids), and jam away. Your first song? How about "Row, Row, Row Your Boat"? **Tip:** You can sharpen your chops by employing a piece of flexible plastic tubing. Rather than try to move your mouth from bottle to bottle, hold one end of the tube in your mouth and move the other end from bottle to bottle.

The Major Scale
Do — 7 ounces
Re — 9½ ounces
Mi — 12½ ounces
Fa — 14 ounces
So — 16½ ounces
La — 17½ ounces
Ti — 18½ ounces
Do — 19 ounces

"Row, Row, Row Your Boat"
1 1 1 2 3
3 2 3 4 5
8 8 8 5 5 5 3 3 3 1 1 1
5 4 3 2 1

Listen to a Rain Stick

142 In South America, craftsmen press thorns into the hollow shaft of a dried-out ocotillo cactus and then fill it with small stones. When the stick is turned upside down, the pebbles cascade over the thorns, creating the magical sound of rain falling on leaves. Your child can make a musical rain stick of his own — from a cardboard mailing tube and dry rice or beans.

MATERIALS

½ **pound of finishing nails and a hammer**

Cardboard mailing tube

1 to 2 cups of small beans or rice

Tape

Acrylic paint and paintbrushes

Randomly hammer nails into the sides of the cardboard mailing tube. Ideally, the nails should be almost as long as the tube is wide.

With one end of the tube

securely capped (tape if necessary), pour the beans or rice into the cylinder. Then place a hand over its open end and tilt the tube to test the sound. You can pour out some of the filler or add more until you achieve the sound you like. (If you want a slower-sounding fall, hammer in more nails.) Cap the open end and tape.

Now decorate the outside of the rain stick with acrylic paint. Once the paint dries completely, tilt the stick, close your eyes, and listen to the rain fall.

Tape Recorder Time

143 Speaking — or singing! — into a tape recorder is in itself lots of fun, but playing back the tape is the real hoot. Try one of these great tape capers.

Name That Noise: Kids record sounds (Fido snoring, the faucet dripping), and parents must guess them.

News Broadcast: Kids get the scoop, interviewing family members about breakfast, the new bunk bed, the arrival of spring …

Stuffies Tell All: Beanies make up the guest panel in this talk show that, of course, requires kids to play both parts.

Play a Kazoo

144 Here are three handy – and impressive – sound effects every kazooist should practice.

Mosquito: Make a high, steady *eeeee* sound. Punctuate with crescendos and lower pitches for realism.

Motorcycle: Growl and flutter your tongue a bit, or try *brroom, brrum.* Add a small explosion for emphasis.

Foghorn: Say a long, low *baahh.* Pause, repeat.

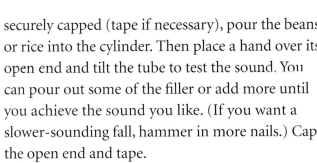

Rainy Days

Decorate an Umbrella

145 Your child can stay dry *and* make a big splash with a hand-painted umbrella.

MATERIALS

Solid-color nylon umbrella

Pencil or soft chalk

Foam paintbrushes
    (1 narrow, 1 broad)

Fabric paint

Use the pencil or chalk to outline a design on the open umbrella, then use the narrow brush to paint over the outline and the broad brush to fill in larger shapes. Let the paint dry thoroughly, then head happily into the rain. Try the easy ladybug and cowgirl we show here, or one of the designs below.

Night sky: Use a stamp to decorate a navy blue or black umbrella with stars.

The solar system: Paint on a golden sun surrounded by all the planets in orbit.

Full bloom: Create a gardenful of colorful flowers or one giant sunflower.

Rose-colored Windows

"On a gray day last year, to help cheer things up and satisfy our longing for flowers, we used washable paints (see page 142 for a recipe) to paint some on a window. Danielle, age six, and David, four, used paintbrushes and their fingers to make the stems, leaves, and different flower blossoms, while Jonathan, two, finger-painted the grass all along the bottom. Our row of brightly colored flowers was so beautiful that we kept it on the window even after our real flowers had blossomed outside." — Christine Nowaczyk, Midland, Michigan

Cloud Nines

147 One way to brighten a rainy day is to dish up a tropical treat: sunny pineapple slices peeking out from behind a big, billowy marshmallow-cream cloud.

INGREDIENTS

1/2	pint heavy cream
	A few grains of salt
1	teaspoon pineapple juice
1/4	teaspoon vanilla extract
2	cups mini marshmallows
	Fresh or canned pineapple slices

In a chilled stainless steel mixing bowl, combine the heavy cream, salt, pineapple juice, and vanilla extract. Whip until soft peaks form. Fold in the mini marshmallows, cover, and refrigerate for at least 1 hour. (The marshmallows will sweeten the cream as it sets.)

Just before serving, trim the outer edges of the pineapple slices to resemble sun rays. Place each pineapple slice in the center of a plate and top with a generous dollop of marshmallow cream. Serves 6 to 8.

Splash Dance

146 Surprise your kids by encouraging their singin' and dancin' in the rain. Let them don their swimsuits, or get soaked to the skin in their clothes (they'll dry, after all!). Play some music out the window to inspire this age-old celebration of precipitation.

93

CRAFT FUN

Lollipop Flowers

148 When it comes to brightening up a rainy day, there's nothing quite like flower power. To make a cheery bouquet of treats, cut petals and leaves from colored paper and affix them to lollipops with tape. For a blossoming centerpiece, insert the lollipop stems into a Styrofoam dome (sold at most craft stores).

MUD FUN
Make the Mud Parfait or Pie à la Mud on page 103, or play Stuck in the Mud, page 102.

KITCHEN FUN

Rainy-day Cake

149 Someone left the cake out in the rain — and we mean that in a good way! Our fun frosting projects brings sunshine to even the dreariest afternoon.

INGREDIENTS

- 1 baked 9- by 13-inch cake
  White frosting
  Food coloring
  Pastry bag fitted with icing tips

Ice the cooled cake. Divide the remaining icing into five small bowls and mix in food coloring (we used red, orange, yellow, green, and blue). Spoon the desired color into a pastry bag (place the coupler base into the bag first, then the frosting, then roll the bag down so the frosting goes into the bottom). Attach the desired tip by

Tip: Twist the opening of the pastry bag shut to keep the frosting from spilling out. Squeeze the bag from the top to push the frosting out through the tip.

screwing on the coupler ring.

To create a rainy-day scene, use a drawing tip to outline clouds, a sun, raindrops, grass, and a simple figure holding an umbrella. For the best results, wash out the tip each time you switch colors. To make flowers, use a star tip for the petals and a leaf tip for leaves. With the tip of your choice, pipe a border around the whole scene, if desired. Serves 10 to 12.

A Shower of Ideas

150 One month's rain brings the next month's flowers — and plenty of chances for kids to get their feet wet with these activities.

✦ Scout out a salamander parade (see "I Spy Salamanders" on page 106 for tips).

✦ Size up raindrops — they range from smaller than a pinhead to as big as a pencil eraser. Catch some in a pan filled with 2 inches of flour, let the flour pellets dry, then compare them.

✦ Draw a tree trunk on a paper plate in crayon. With washable colored markers, top the trunk with bold squiggles. Then hold the plate in the rain and watch the "leaves" unfurl.

✦ Conduct a rain symphony by setting an array of pots, bottoms up, below a dripping roof edge.

FUN FACT A falling raindrop is not pear-shaped. Most raindrops flatten as they fall and are shaped like hamburger buns.

Watercolor Chalk Painting

151 During a gentle rainfall, hand your kids some colored chalk and let them create an impressionistic masterpiece. They can draw rainbows, family portraits, and nature scenes on the driveway, then watch the rain blur the edges (big, simple images produce the best results). To help the rain along, "paint" over the picture with a large, damp paintbrush.

Blooming Good Fun

"My four-year-old daughter's love of flowers inspired a great rainy-day activity. When she and her twin brother feel housebound, we head for our local greenhouse. The twins are free to wander through the large, open areas, protected from the weather, and enjoy the wonderful colors, scents, and textures. They also have fun seeing how the plants grow from tiny seedlings and watching the florists make beautiful arrangements. My son is especially intrigued by the hose and sprinkler system used for watering. And if you can bear to leave without making a purchase, the whole thing is free!"
— Linda B. Jennings, Hackettstown, New Jersey

CHAPTER FIVE

The Four Seasons

When boredom strikes, step outside and let nature work its magic

Wherever your family lives, the seasons offer a year's worth of outdoor adventures. Maybe you go apple picking every fall. Come winter, you build snowmen in the backyard and sip mugs of hot chocolate. Spring means May Day baskets to decorate the neighborhood, and summer's warmth brings long days of towering sand castles.

For many of us, these seasonal pastimes have become rituals — activities our children anticipate as the weather changes. These traditions are touch points: they help us mark the passing of time, and even slow it down just a little. They thrill us with anticipation and then comfort us with their familiarity.

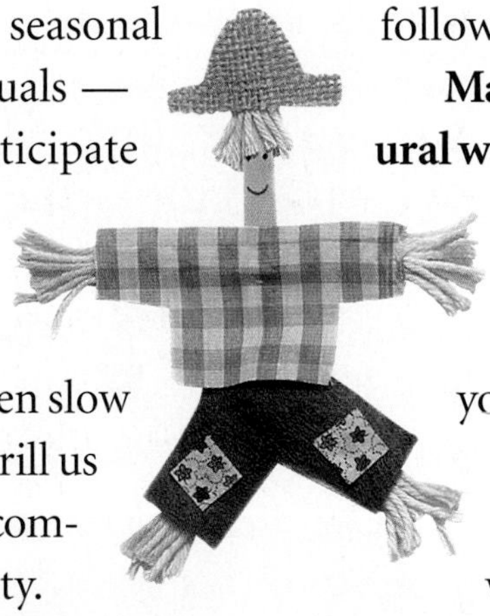

And, as every parent knows, seasonal activities keep our children naturally busy. In the great outdoors, they are entertained by nature. A beach becomes a giant sandbox. An open field with wildflowers and overturned logs becomes a playground. When we attune

our kids to the rhythms of nature, we offer sweet relief from the intrusions and constraints of schedules, TV, and even heaps of toys and games. Dawn and moonrise, spring and fall: natural cycles nurture a kid's creativity in fun, often unexpected ways.

On the following pages, you and your family will discover countless ways to celebrate each season. As you peruse our crafts and activities, consider the following tips:

Make the most of what the natural world has to offer. Snow, mud, sand, and leaves — these natural playthings have timeless appeal to kids. Offer your children plenty of opportunities to play with smooth sticks, skipping stones, even weathered hunks of driftwood. These humble bits of nature will capture your kids' imaginations.

Go on a seasonal scavenger hunt. Those same natural goodies that beg to be played with also beg to be collected. Give your kids a list of nature items to find and a lunch-size paper

Mini Scarecrow, page 123

Paint a Fall Mural, page 127

bag. Or you can simply hand them a field guide and a pair of binoculars. Anything you see can be sketched or painted; gathered items can be made into crafts.

Take a hike. Grab a walking stick (see page 124), pick a favorite route, and walk it at least once each season. Encourage your kids to attend to the shifting landscape, the absent or reappearing wildlife, and which views become more or less prominent. Keep a nature journal (see our Beat-a-leaf Journal on page 152) to record your observations from season to season and year to year. Or make a seasonal photo album and use it to document the changing scenery — and your changing kids.

Grow a garden. There may be no better way to understand the rhythms of nature: bulbs planted in the fall will send up shoots in the spring; tomato seeds pushed deep into spring's chilly soil will bear heavy fruit come summertime. Even the winter offers indoor gardeners a crack at sprouting some greenery. In the dark days of winter, this bit of color can really invigorate the senses.

Seasonal Classics

Fall: Pick apples, plant bulbs, carve pumpkins, collect leaves, mull cider, dry gourds for rattles
Winter: Go sledding, play ice hockey, make a snow angel, drink hot cocoa, cook a giant pot of soup
Spring: Make mud pies, splash in puddles, plant seeds, visit baby animals, dig for worms, dye eggs
Summer: Build sand castles, freeze Popsicles, play Marco Polo, go to a fair, make a daisy chain, pick berries for jam

Spring

Run Like the Wind

153 With its breezy long tail, this toy will make any kid feel like he's flying. Cut the bottoms off two large plastic cups. Lay a large, clear trash bag flat and roll its bottom end around the outside of one cup. Tape in place about an inch below its rim. Feed the trash bag through the bottom of the second cup and nest this cup firmly over the first. Fringe the tail of the trash bag with scissors and punch opposing holes through both cups just below the rims. Push a dowel through the holes and secure it with a rubber band. Run like the wind!

RECYCLED CRAFT

Whirly Bottles

152 Celebrate spring by planting a row of spinning wind catchers in your front yard.

MATERIALS

- 2-liter plastic soda bottle
- Colored marker, paper, and tape
- Craft knife
- Acrylic paints and paintbrushes
- Power drill, hammer, and a small nail
- 3 feet of 1-inch-diameter wooden dowel

First, remove the label from the bottle. This is easier if you fill the bottle with hot water and let it sit for 10 minutes. Then use soapy water and a vegetable scrubber to remove any glue. Drain the bottle and let it dry.

Ask your child to come up with a decorative image to paint on the bottle, then make a template by drawing the design on paper. If she chooses a symmetrical image, such as a butterfly or flower, have her draw a straight line down the center of her drawing and cut out one half of the image. If it's an animal, draw a profile of its head and neck.

Tape the template onto the inverted bottle. Use the marker to trace around its outer edge (do not trace the centerline or the base of the neck). Repeat this step a few times, keeping an equal amount of space between the outlines. Use the craft knife to cut along the outlines (adults only). Fold the silhouettes forward at a 90-degree angle from the bottle. Now paint the images. Once the paint dries, drill a small hole in the center of the bottle bottom (adults only). Insert the dowel into the bottle. Tap the nail through the hole in the bottom and into the top of the dowel so that the head extends ¼ inch above the plastic.

NEIGHBORHOOD FUN

Spring Scavenger Hunt

154 Clues of the season's arrival come in many forms. Give kids a list of spring signs to hunt for, including sounds (like peepers, the knocking of a woodpecker, a bird singing), plant life (a tree bud, a mushroom), critters (a salamander, a baby animal, a turtle on a log), or human hints (a baby out in a stroller, laundry hanging out to dry, someone on a skateboard), and send your kids out into the sun. Players get a point for every sign of spring they find. The winner is crowned Super Spring Sleuth.

KITCHEN FUN

Let's Go Eat a Kite

155 If there's a stiff breeze aloft, head for a rolling field and catch it — with a kite. After everyone's worked up an appetite sailing, swooping, and loop-the-looping, serve kite-shaped sandwiches that are guaranteed to elicit smiles all around, no strings attached.

INGREDIENTS

1 piece of firm bread
  Peanut butter
  Jelly
  Carrot, peeled

First, trim the edges of the bread to create an elongated diamond and place it on a plate. Spread peanut butter and jelly in a decorative pattern, as shown. Next, use a vegetable peeler to shave a long, thin strip from the side of the carrot. Curl the shaving into a kite tail and tuck one end under the lower corner of the bread. Place it on a blue plate, if you have one, to simulate a clear, sunny sky. Cut the rest of the carrot into sticks to eat with the sandwich. Serves 1.

FUN FACT You might be blown away to learn that the world's windiest place is Antarctica, where winds regularly gust at more than 60 mph.

HOMEMADE TOY

Wind Bags

156 Throw your grocery bag to the wind with this kite-flying feat. First, tie together the handles of a plastic shopping bag with the end of a ball of string. Staple a few 2-foot lengths of ribbon to the bottom of the bag for kite tails. Now find a windy spot outdoors and start running. As the bag fills with air, slowly let out the string and the kite should begin to soar and dive.

INSTANT FUN
Blow a Blade of Grass

157 Nothing heralds the arrival of summer quite like a blast from a blade of grass played between the thumbs. In the hands of one kid, it's a trumpet fanfare. In the hands of another, it's more like the honk of a man blowing his nose. No matter. The fun is more in the playing than the listening. With a blade of grass and a little know-how, anyone can grasp the technique.

First, find a nice, wide blade of grass at least 3 inches long. Lick the edge of one thumb from wrist to tip and stick the blade of grass where you've licked (it's gross, we know, but the moisture keeps the grass from falling off). Carefully press your two hands together, as if in prayer, lining up your thumbs so that

they sandwich the grass at the top knuckle and at the base of your palms, with a gap in between. Wiggle your thumbs until the grass bisects the gap, put your lips to your thumbs, and blow through the hole.

FUN FACT When you blow a blade of grass between your thumbs, you're using the same physics employed by modern reed instruments, such as clarinets. In each case, blown air causes a thin blade, or reed, to vibrate, creating sound.

INSTANT FUN
Spring Picnic

158 Keep a "just add food" picnic basket packed, and you can lunch alfresco at the drop of a blanket. Simply stock a wicker basket with paper plates, plastic cups, forks, and spoons, napkins, a tablecloth, salt and pepper shakers, and a Frisbee. Then just add food and go!

PORCH DECORATION
Wind Dancer

159 The next time a warm breeze starts to stir, hang up one of these foam wind socks and watch the ribbon streamers start to dance. To assemble one, use a hole punch to make five holes along one shorter end of a 4$^{1}/_{2}$- by 12-inch piece of craft foam. Roll the foam into a tube, overlapping the edges, and punch matching holes in the other end. Lace the two ends together with ribbon. Next, punch a series of holes along the lower edge of the sock and tie a long ribbon from each one. Then make two holes in the top and tie on a ribbon for hanging. Lastly, lace on cutout foam flowers through holes punched in the sock.

Stuck in the Mud

160 After a long, cold winter, we don't warm to a game with a name like "freeze tag." Try this springtime variation on the classic.

What you need:

Three or more players

How to play: Choose someone to be "It." His name is Mud. To start, each player takes hold of one of Mr. (or Ms.) Mud's fingers, and all chant, "What happened to you, Mr. Mud, while spring flowers, they did bud?!" Then, at an unpredictable speed — the point is to trick the players — Mr. Mud chants back, "I slipped into the crud! I got stuck in the ... mud!" At the sound of the word *mud*, all the players let go of Mr. Mud's fingers and scatter away while he gives chase. If Mr. Mud tags a player, that player is "stuck in the mud" (that is, frozen). The sole way to get unstuck is for an untagged player to crawl under the stuck player's legs. Players are safe only while they are in those crawling-under moments. You play until everyone is caught. Then name another Mud and begin again.

Prepare a Mud Parfait

161 Mired in mud? Let your children make the most of it with our elegant twist on the classic mud pie. Make the parfait glass (see below) several hours before heading for the mud, to allow the glue time to dry. Your mud chefs can collect parfait ingredients, such as leaves, twigs, or pebbles, while they wait.

MATERIALS

Rubber band

Clear 2-liter bottle with cap

Craft knife or scissors

Craft Goop (or other glue made for plastics)

Mud, pebbles, leaves, and other ingredients

Using a rubber band around the bottle as a guide, cut around the bottle about 4 inches from the bottom (a parent's job).

Trim the base section again just above the molded ridges. Discard the center portion.

Turn the top and bottom parts upside down and glue the cap onto the center of the base.

When the glue's dry, your child can fill it trifle style — alternating layers of mud with pebbles, sand, dirt, leaves, and any other ingredients she likes. Top with a rock cherry and a leaf.

Enjoy a Pie à la Mud

162 To make an edible counterpart to the muddy creation above, spread a store-bought chocolate cookie piecrust with ½ quart of softened chocolate ice cream. Dig eight holes in the ice cream and fill each with a tablespoon of fudge topping. Freeze until firm. Stir ½ cup of chocolate chip rocks into ½ quart of ice cream and spread over the pie. Top with chocolate whipped cream (¼ cup of hot-cocoa mix beaten with 1 cup of heavy cream) and chocolate cookie crumb dirt. Freeze until serving time.

Gumdrop Garden

163 This spring, plant a row of candy tulips in a cake-and-cookie garden. First, ice the top and sides of a pound cake with chocolate frosting, then trim a row of ladyfingers to make a picket fence. Sprinkle on chocolate cookie crumbs for soil. Use kitchen scissors to snip flattened gumdrops into tulips. Trim flattened green gumdrops into leaves, and use toothpicks to attach the leaves and flowers to the cake. Finally, tint coconut with green food coloring to make yummy grass.

May Day Bouquets

164 Create a buzz by hanging these easy May Day baskets on all your neighbors' doorknobs.

MATERIALS

- **Construction paper**
- **Tape or stapler**
- **Pipe cleaners**
- **Pom-poms**
- **Glue**
- **Googly eyes**
- **Feathers**

Hold a sheet of construction paper (black for the bee, yellow for the duck) with the shorter ends at the top and bottom. Starting at the lower right-hand corner, roll the sheet into a cone and tape or staple the overlap. Trim the top front to create a rounded head on the front side.

To make a bee, the next step is to form antennae. Fold a pipe cleaner in half, stapling the bend to the back of the head. Curl each tip around a black pom-pom.

Next, create stripes by wrapping strips of yellow paper around the cone and gluing them in place. Tape on paper wings and a heart-shaped paper face complete with a drawn mouth and glued-on pom-pom eyeballs topped with googly-eye pupils. For a hanger, make holes in opposite sides of the cone a half inch from the top. Thread a

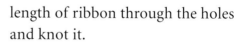

length of ribbon through the holes and knot it.

To make the duck, cut out wings, a broad breast feather, and webbed feet from construction paper. Tape the pieces in place. Glue tail feathers to the tip of the cone and googly eyes to the head. Finally, cut out a bill from a folded piece of orange paper, using the fold for the top edge. Attach the bottom flap to the cone, then glue a pair of mini pom-pom nostrils to the top.

A Doorstep Garden

165 You don't need window boxes to spruce up your front yard with spring flowers. Just plant your favorite annuals in an old boot to set beside a welcome mat. Remove the lace from the boot and fill its bottom with a layer of pebbles or gravel to provide drainage, then pack in a 2-inch layer of potting soil. Now fit in the root base of a small flowering plant (pansies, marigolds, or impatiens work well), and gently pack more soil around and on top of the roots.

Pal Around

166 With warming temperatures, Little League games, and school vacation just weeks away, springtime puts friends in the mood to kick up their heels. Here are a few suggestions for ushering in a spring of good company:

Go into business (selling cookies and pink lemonade, delivering groceries, or dog walking) and design flyers to post in your neighborhood.

Pack a picnic lunch (see page 101), spread a blanket on the grass, then sit back and watch the clouds roll by.

Plant a friendship garden full of your favorite flowers. After they bloom, try drying them, then make cards to swap with friends.

Go strawberry picking at a local farm, then get help cooking the berries down into a thick syrup or jam to top your post-sleepover pancakes.

A Pick-and-eat Garden

167 A pick-and-eat garden is fast food at its healthiest, boredom-busting best. Look for varieties that can go from vine to table with just a quick wash.

Peas: Try compact varieties that don't require trellising, like Sugar Ann.

Pole beans: Kentucky Wonder and Kentucky Blue are both dependable varieties that produce long, tender beans. Create a tepee of bamboo stakes for them to climb.

Cherry tomatoes: We like Super Sweet 100 because it's easy for small hands to harvest. Plant in cages, or stake.

Radishes: Kids may find them too spicy to eat, but few crops grow faster. Plus, it's fun to yank them from the earth. We like the Easter Egg II variety.

Tin Man

168 Looking for a garden sentry that's worth crowing about? This one is well equipped to ruffle some feathers — particularly if they're about to light on your vegetable patch.

MATERIALS

7 feet of 2- by 3-inch wooden stud

4 feet of 3¼-inch dowel

4 large brass hooks

Twine

Assorted hardware, kitchen utensils, and clothing (see below)

Glue

First, set one end of the wooden stud 18 inches into the ground. Next, cut two pieces of dowel to measure 3 feet long and 1 foot long. Screw hooks into the ends of both dowels. With twine, securely tie the longer dowel to the stud about 10 inches from the top, as shown. Hang metal spatula forearms from the hooks and use safety pins to attach metal measuring-spoon fingers to the spatulas. Tie on the shorter dowel 18 inches below the top one. Then loop leg-length pieces of twine around the hooks on the short dowel.

Now dress the scarecrow in jeans, using suspenders to hang them from the shoulder dowel. Thread the twine through the legs and tie saucepan boots to the ends. Button on a flappy shirt.

For a head, fit an inverted metal coffeepot atop the stud and glue on washers for eyes. Tie a bandanna around the neck. To cap it all off, use wire to firmly fasten a metal colander hat to the coffeepot handle and then attach measuring spoons for hair.

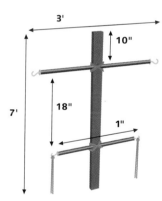

I Spy Salamanders

Spring showers trigger an annual parade of salamanders marching to ponds to lay their eggs. The following conditions lend themselves to amphibian-spotting: warm, wet weather; the muted light of dusk; roads that border wetlands. Ask your town conservation commission if it knows of a favorite salamander crossing.

FIELD TRIP
Visit a Farm
170 Even while your kids are waiting to shed their parkas, farms are coming to life with litters of newborns. Visit a farm in early spring, and you may get to bottle-feed a tiny pink piglet (one from a litter of more than a dozen!) or a snowy lamb. Goats butt their way into the world a little later In the season, and with any luck, calves, foals, chicks, and kittens may also be included in the spring mix. An added bonus: farms tend to be friendly and free! Look in your phone book for a farm associated with an agricultural college or a vocational school.

NATURE CRAFT
Sprout Necklace

169 Our all-natural necklace requires daily attention to thrive, but it rewards its caretaker with a real live sprout, suitable for transplanting to a pot and growing in a sunny window. The necklace itself, we should note, also serves as an attractive spring fashion accessory.

MATERIALS

- **Small screw eye**
- **Small clear plastic jar with a cap (like those for spices, vitamins, or cake decorations)**
- **3 one-yard lengths of colorful string**
- **3 cotton balls**
- **3 or 4 dried beans (like kidney, pinto, or lima)**

Carefully twist the screw eye into the center of the jar lid (create a pilot hole with a pushpin if necessary).

Braid the colored string, thread it through the screw eye, and tie the ends, making sure the loop can fit over your head.

Moisten the cotton balls until they are wet but not dripping and place them in the jar. Press the beans down between the jar wall and the cotton so they are clearly visible from the outside. Screw on the cap.

Wear your sprout necklace during the day, keeping it out of direct sunlight to avoid overheating. Store it in a warm place at night. After about five days, the beans should begin to sprout. When they begin to crowd the jar, transplant them to a flowerpot, or discard them and start a new batch.

Tip: Under normal conditions, the cotton should not dry out, but check it periodically and add more water if it does.

Ants on a Log

171 These critters make a welcome addition to any picnic. First, scrape a flat spot on the bottoms of 12 chocolate malt balls. Melt 1/2 cup of chocolate chips in a double boiler. Set four pretzel rods on a wire rack, drizzle on melted chocolate, then press three malt balls, flat sides down, on each pretzel. For legs, use six chow mein noodles dipped into the chocolate. Use chocolate to attach candy dot eyes and licorice antennae.

Bug Hotel

172 They show up every spring, flying into town and banging on our screens as if we owed them a room for the night. Well, here's hospitality everyone can live with. Our bug hotel is simple yet sturdy, with lots of observation windows for young entomologists. Guests check in, then you get to check 'em out.

MATERIALS

> Oatmeal container
>
> Markers or poster paint and paintbrushes
>
> Craft knife
>
> 2 feet of fiberglass screening (from a hardware store)

Use markers or poster paint to decorate the outside of the oatmeal container, making sure you post the house rules!

Paint or draw the shutters, then use a craft knife (adults only) to cut them out with sideways H shapes.

Paint the door, then cut it out, making sure its bottom edge is at least ¼ inch above the floor inside (to keep your captured "guests" from checking out too early).

Roll the screening around the inside of the container so it fits snugly. Trim it so the top edge fits beneath the lid and leave a 1-inch overlap where the side edges meet.

Tip: Be sure to provide your guests with food (notice what they were eating when you found them) and water (a filled plastic bottle cap should meet their needs).

Terra-cotta Birdbath

173 A fresh, clean source of water can be hard for birds to come by. That's why a birdbath is a great device for attracting all kinds of species, such as catbirds, wrens, waxwings, even screech owls. Here's one that couldn't be simpler to put together.

MATERIALS

- 2 unglazed pot trays, one 8¼ inches in diameter and one 12¼ inches in diameter
- Unglazed clay pot, 6 inches in diameter
- Permanent enamel satin-finish paint (we recommend Delta CeramDecor's PermEnamel air-drying nontoxic paint)
- Paintbrushes
- Clear satin-finish enamel glaze

First, invert the smaller clay tray and the pot on a newspaper-covered surface so your child can paint a decorative design on the stand. (Don't paint the larger tray, though: the unpainted surface will provide a better grip for visiting birds.) Let the paint dry thoroughly. For added durability, seal the stand with a coat of clear glaze.

To assemble the birdbath, invert the pot on the small tray for the stand, then set the larger tray right side up atop the pot. Fill your birdbath with no more than 3 inches of water.

Wrangle Some Worms

174 This see-through ranch allows kids to watch earthworms tunneling. Fill a 1-gallon clear glass or plastic jar with potting soil that you've mixed with about 6 cups of manure. Moisten the soil well with water. Now gather up about a half dozen worms (they're easiest to spot after a rain) and add them to your container. Cover the jar with a screen, or punch plenty of airholes in its lid. Now tape black construction paper around the jar — worms like the dark — and set your ranch in a cool, shady place. Keep the soil moist. In a few days, remove the paper and look for worm tunnels down the side of the jar: the worms are hard at work digesting dirt! When you're all done spying on them, release the worms into your garden.

Early Bird Special

175 Even a child who usually pecks at her breakfast will find this tasty nest hard to resist. Grease a large muffin cup with butter. Let your child crush two Shredded Wheat biscuits and set them aside. Melt 1 tablespoon of butter in a small saucepan over medium heat. Add ¼ cup of Marshmallow Fluff. Continue to cook, stirring constantly. As soon as the mixture starts to bubble, remove it from the heat and stir in the crushed cereal until it is well coated. Press the mixture into the greased mold in a nest shape. Let it harden. Remove it from the mold and place it in a serving bowl. Fill with fresh berries and milk. Serves 1.

Summer

OUTDOOR ACTIVITIES

Fun in the Sun

176 Make the most of these long, warm days with a summertime-only activity:

- Race the sun by trying to eat a Popsicle before it melts
- Pick blueberries from a farm, then make a pie or a jar of jam
- Team up around the clothesline for an impromptu volleyball match
- Hose off the dog
- Stay up late and watch the stars come out

CRAFT FUN

Memory Box

177 One way your child can treasure her summer memories is by collecting all kinds of mementos in, and on, a special box.

MATERIALS

> Plain box, shoe box, or photo box with a cover
>
> Adhesives (a glue stick or double-sided tape for flat, lightweight objects; tacky glue or a low-temperature glue gun for heavier objects)
>
> Colored permanent markers

Throughout the summer school vacation, as she collects ticket stubs, postcards, trinkets, stickers, or any other paraphernalia, your child can either glue them to the outside of the box or store them inside. She can even add a note in colored marker about where or when she came by a certain item.

FUN FACT The phrase "dog days of summer" was coined 2,500 years ago after the Dog Star, Sirius, visible in the Northern Hemisphere by mid-July. The ancient Greeks believed its light caused temperatures to soar. Sirius does burn almost twice as hotly as our sun, but it's much too far away to have any effect on the earth's climate.

Sights of Summer

178 To savor your kids' sunny days of free play, compile a list of classic sights of summer and see how many they can scope out and photograph with a disposable camera. Here are some ideas: Black-eyed Susans ✦ Watermelons, tomatoes, beans, or other summer harvest fruits or vegetables ✦ Dragonfly, ladybug, or praying mantis ✦ Kids running through the sprinkler ✦ Starfish, sand castle, and seaweed ✦ Garter snake ✦ Fishing pole ✦ Tennis racket ✦ A favorite tree in full bloom ✦ Summer-reading book cover

Bake a Sunshine Cake

179 A summer birthday or dinner party calls for a dessert that's all sweetness and light — like this glittery sunburst cake.

INGREDIENTS

- 2 8- or 9-inch round baked cakes
  Yellow frosting
- 7 to 9 sugar cones
  Yellow crystallized sugar

Frost the top of one cake, then add the second layer and frost the entire cake. Ice the outside of one cone and roll it in the sugar. Push the open end into the side of the cake, using more frosting to hold it in place, if needed. Repeat with the other cones, positioning them around the cake like sunrays.

Sun Catchers

180 When you hang these translucent shapes in a window, the marker colors light up like stained glass. To begin, your child should use a black permanent marker to draw the outline of a picture or geometric shape on a soft, clear plastic lid, such as that from a coffee can. Cut out the shape with scissors (a parent's job), then have your child completely fill in the shape with colored permanent markers. Punch a hole in the top of the shape, tie on a loop of string or fishing line, and hang your sun catcher from the top of a window.

Backyard Camp-out

182 Sure, we like acres of land, flickering fireflies, and the howl of distant coyotes, but all the space you really need for a wild camp-out is a suburban backyard, a city rooftop, or a nearby grassy field.

WHAT YOU NEED

   Tent

   Sleeping bags

   Flashlights and battery-
      operated lanterns

Kids and grown-ups can set up the campsite nice and early, then the grown-ups can order a pizza and scuttle away inside to let the kids go it alone in the great backyard — until s'more time! After dessert, the kids can make shadow puppets on the tent wall, turn off the lights for ghost stories, or lie outside on their backs and watch the constellations pass by. Come morning, greet your brave campers with hot chocolate and a hearty pancake breakfast.

KITCHEN FUN

Simple S'mores

181 Summer just wouldn't be complete if you didn't get your fill of the classic campfire dessert — a warm and gooey s'more. To sample this supersimple double-chocolate version, toast a marshmallow to golden perfection, sandwich it between chocolate-covered graham crackers, squish, and eat.

INSTANT FUN

Shadow Puppet Show

183 Hand shadows projected on the tent wall by flashlight add a spooky touch to your ghost stories. To create a dog's face, hold you hands in the shape shown at right. Move your fingers to make the dog look as if it's talking. For bigger shadows, move your hands closer to the light. Now make up a shadowy tale about a ghost dog that haunts the tent, the sleeping bags, and even the campers.

Ship Ahoy!

184 If landlocked boredom's got your kids walking the plank, let them turn a refrigerator box on its side and chill out on the salty waves of their imagination.

MATERIALS

Blue tarp

Large appliance box

Clothesline and sheet

Assorted props

Spread out the tarp and set the box on it, on its side, underneath a clothesline. Open up — or cut away — the top side of the box (only parents should use a craft knife). Now drape a sheet sail over the line, assemble some themed props, and it's anchors away!

Fishing trip: Bring a tackle box and wooden-dowel fishing rods, construction paper fish, snorkels, and worms!

Pirate ship: Grab bandannas, a stuffed parrot, eye patches, broom oars, striped leggings, and a black flag with a skull and crossbones.

Yacht: Have pretend pipes, sailing caps, blazers, fancy snacks, and juice in plastic wineglasses.

Tour Your Hometown

185 Who says you have to go away to have a special family vacation? With a little creativity and imagination (you do, after all, have to pretend you're a tourist), you can have a memorable getaway without ever leaving town.

- Call your chamber of commerce or visitors' bureau for local brochures and maps to area attractions.

- Take a nature walk at a local park, conservation area, or reservoir.

- Consider hopping aboard a local train, bus, trolley, or subway — for the pure fun of it.

- Ask the fire station, bakery, or a local factory if your family can have a tour.

- Visit a college campus. You'll find athletic fields for playing baseball and flying kites. You might also find museums, sporting events, theater, and arcades in the student centers (a treat to kids, at least).

Swing on a Tire

186 Endlessly entertaining, all but indestructible, and virtually free. The tire swing is all three — and a vintage icon of summertime to boot! If one doesn't already hang in your backyard, the situation is easily corrected, but keep in mind these safety tips from a playground safety expert.

- The best tire is a used, beltless, light-truck tire (ask for one at a tire store or junkyard). Avoid steel-belted tires, whose sharp cords might work to the surface.
- Hang the swing from a hardwood tree, such as a

sugar maple, oak, or beech. Avoid soft-limbed evergreens and fast-growing species such as silver maple and willow.

- Choose a healthy branch that's at least 8 inches in diameter. The higher the branch, the longer the swing's arc.
- Suspend the tire with rot-proof nylon rope.
- Drill drainage holes in the bottom of the tire.
- Put wood chips, pine bark, or some other soft material beneath and around the swing to cushion falls.

Float the Day Away

187 Spending a day tubing down a gentle river is like getting a free pass to nature's own waterpark. As uncomplicated as the fun is, there are some things to keep in mind:

◆ Take two cars and drop off one where you plan to get out.

◆ Ask others about hazards or scout the river beforehand.

◆ The best tubes are from old trucks or tractors (ask for them at farm-supply or tire stores), but wrap the metal valve stem in foam rubber, then duct-tape it to the side of the tube so it doesn't scratch you. (Smaller kids can use snow tubes.)

◆ Wear old sneakers (or other foot protection), sunscreen and maybe even a hat, and — most important — life jackets.

◆ To float as a group, leash the tubes together with rope.

◆ After tubing, shuttle a driver back to the car at the starting point.

The Water Purse

188 Talk about wash and wear! This easy-to-make waterproof drawstring purse, crafted from an onion bag, is more than just a fashion statement. Secured to your clothing with a plastic clip, it's invaluable for carrying quarters for the pool's soda machine or hauling your goggles and earplugs to the beach. Just weave a length of plastic twine around the onion bag's opening to serve as a drawstring. About halfway around the bag, weave the twine through the loop of a plastic clip, like the kind commonly sold as key chains.

Sunflyer

190 Your child won't need a green thumb to make this sunflower wind dancer burst with vivid color — just a plateful of her favorite buttons. Start by snipping triangles from the rim of a large yellow plastic plate to create flower petals. Next, invert a paper plate, center it on top of the yellow one, and glue it into position. Once the paper plate has dried in place, glue on buttons of various colors and sizes, enough to cover the white surface. Attach a loop of thin ribbon to the back rim of the yellow plate to use as a hanger. Finally, glue on green ribbons (each about 2 feet long) so they fly from the bottom.

Weave a Daisy Crown

189 Funny how you can pack your summer full of activities and your kids will remember one thing: sitting with you on the edge of a field, weaving together daisy chains. In case you didn't catch the directions back when you were a flower child, here they are:

Pick a slew of daisies or dandelions with stems at least a few inches long. Each child needs about 25.

With a sharp knife (parents only), make a ¼-inch slit in each stem, 2 inches below the blossom. Slip the next flower's stem through the slit and pull it until you get to the flower head. Do the same with the next daisy and the next until you've made a chain the right length for your child's head.

Turn the chain into a crown by twisting the last stem around the first. If your stems are very long, you can intertwine them to make the crown more secure.

Dried Flowers

191 Preserving summer pansies or violets is a cinch with this method. Mix 1 part powdered borax with 2 parts cornmeal and fill a small cardboard box with a ¾-inch layer of the mixture. Place the flower blossoms facedown in the box, then cover them with another ¾-inch layer of the mixture. Store the box with the lid on at room temperature for three to four weeks, or until the petals are completely dry.

Grow Something Big

192 Gardening, for many kids, would be a whole lot more exciting if growing things didn't take so darn long. The following four varieties, however, shoot up right away in your garden — and then they keep growing, and growing, and growing …

◆ **Atlantic giant pumpkin:** This pale, slightly lumpy pumpkin holds the current world weight record, topping 800 pounds. More typical are 50- and 100-pounders (115 days to maturity).

◆ **Mammoth Russian sunflower:** Flowers grow to 10 inches across on plants more than 10 feet tall (120 days).

◆ **Scarlett runner beans:** You can almost see this climbing vine grow (up to 12 feet), and the purple beans are as pretty as they are tasty (70 to 115 days).

◆ **Morning glory:** Here's another fast-growing vine that rewards gardeners with a show of magnificent blossoms. This one's invasive, so plant it solo (110 to 120 days).

The Four Seasons

Flower Tower in a Bottle

"This summer project began when my five-year-old granddaughter, Brittany, and I bought some sunflower seeds, started them indoors, and then planted them outside. To document how tall her flowers were, we began photographing members of our family for comparison. Soon the plants were bigger than Brittany's sister, Kristin (age three), her cousin Haley (also three), Brittany herself, then her mom, me, her grandfather, and her dad. I put together an album for Brittany that showed the success of her gardening project. It's a nice year-round reminder of our summer fun."

— *Carol Fitzgerald*

WATER FUN

A Beachside Shower

193 Everybody loves spending a fun-packed day at the shore — until it's time to climb back into the car, still sticky and sandy, for the ride home. Here's a quick way for your backseat travelers to freshen up before hitting the road. Fill two or three clean plastic milk jugs with water and leave them in the car while you swim. When you're ready to leave, the water will be warm enough for a soothing rinse.

BEACH CRAFT

Ocean City

194 Your sandy architects can mold a whole seaside metropolis — and then play Godzilla (take a picture first).

MATERIALS

- Shallow, broad-bottomed container (like a bin or a baking pan)
- Cardboard milk carton, with the bottom removed
- Funnel

Use the container as a mold for the ground story of each skyscraper. Pack it with damp sand, invert it onto a flat section of beach, then lift it off.

To erect a second story, set the milk carton upright on the base, fill it halfway with sand, then slowly pour in enough water to dampen it. Repeat, filling to the top with sand, then remove the mold. Top off the building with a sand dome (mold with the funnel) or a stone roof. Finally, press on shell windows and driftwood doors, and arrange beach pebbles into a road.

Tide Pooling

195 You don't have to take your family scuba diving to catch a glimpse of undersea life. Those shallow saltwater pools that form along rocky coastlines are usually teeming with fascinating creatures.

Below you will find a few you're likely to encounter on both the East and West coasts. Remind your children to approach slowly and be very still, lest the animals sense your motion and dart under a rock for cover. And return every animal to its habitat.

Sea cucumbers: A knobby, oblong shape gives these critters their name. They range in color from gray to rose and tend to burrow under the sand.

Sea urchins: Algae are the favorite food of these porcupinelike creatures.

Sand dollars: These flat, disk-shaped animals sport star patterns on their centers and live at the bottom of tide pools.

Hermit crabs: If you

notice a head and claws poking out of a snail shell, it's probably a hermit crab. These crustaceans move into an empty shell (sometimes pulling out the original resident first) to protect their soft abdomens.

Barnacles: These crusty creatures rely on their feathery feet to kick food particles through the valved openings of their bodies.

Starfish: Five arms (and sometimes more) distinguish these creatures. They feed on clams, using the suction cups on their feet to pull open shells.

Sponges: Protruding from the floor and walls of tide pools, sponges are actually large colonies of minuscule animals that eat by sifting food from the ocean water that flows through them.

Art at the Beach

To make the most of your beachcombing finds, consider bringing these supplies:

✦ Fishing line for stringing any shells that have holes

✦ Glue and paper for sand painting

✦ Paper, paint, and paintbrushes to make prints of found objects — seaweed, seashells, sea stars, and so on

✦ Plaster of Paris and a bucket to make casts of footprints in hardpacked sand

✦ Sieves for rinsing shells; bags for storing them

FUN FACT

Do fish sleep? Sort of. All that swimming might make them sleepy, but most fish have no eyelids to close. So they just rest by floating and daydreaming.

Hang a Hideout

196 Call it what you want — a tent, a hideout, a permanent-press playhouse — but a breezy, easy-to-make clothesline fort offers kids ample shade and privacy for tea parties, secret clubs, or just whiling away long afternoons. The construction of the tent is fairly free-form, with its design depending on the length of your clothesline, the size of your yard, and how many sheets you want to use. To make our tent, we strung three clotheslines between a tree and a tall fence (one clothesline runs higher to form the peaked ridgepole of the roof). Then we hung several sheets to form the walls and roof, clipping them in places with clothespins. If your kids like, you can furnish their tent wth kid-size chairs and an old rug — or, as we did, just stick with the original decor by Mother Nature.

Fold Up a Beach Umbrella

197 It's too windy on the beach to read the paper, so you might as well follow these easy directions, adapted from the book *Extra! Extra!: The Who, What, Where, When, and Why of Newspapers,* and recycle those flapping sheets into a shady parasol.

MATERIALS

10 full-size (double) newspaper sheets

Tape

Stapler

Decorative cutouts and fishing line

To make the handle, layer five sheets of newspaper and roll them up diagonally. Tape the roll closed.

To make the stop, roll a sheet of newspaper diagonally into a tube about 2 inches wide and tape the ends. Roll a second sheet the same as the first. Staple the two tubes together at one end and flatten them. Tape one end of this long, flattened tube to the umbrella handle about 2 inches from the top. Wind the long strip around and around until it ends. Tape down the end.

For the canopy, make 1-inch pleats in a sheet of newspaper along its width, like an accordion. Fold the accordion in half. Make two more accordions, fit the three folded accordions together like pieces of a pie, and staple them at all the seams.

To assemble, push the handle of the umbrella up through the center of the canopy. The stop will keep the umbrella top from sliding down or closing. Tape the top to the handle to hold it in place. We decorated ours with metallic fish and cutouts that we strung on with fishing line.

The Four Seasons

Ice Cream in a Bag

198 Forget endlessly cranking the handle of an ice-cream maker. After combining the ingredients, you can shake up your own pouch of soft serve — and it's done in just 5 minutes.

Combine 2 tablespoons of sugar with 1 cup of half and half and 1/2 teaspoon of vanilla extract in a pint-size ziplock bag. Seal it tightly. Place 1/2 cup of salt (kosher or rock salt works best, but table salt is fine) in a gallon-size ziplock bag, and add enough ice cubes to fill the bag halfway. Place the sealed smaller bag inside as well, then seal the larger bag. Now shake the bags until the mixture hardens (about 5 minutes). Feel the small bag to determine when it's done. Take the smaller bag out of the larger one, add mix-ins, and eat the ice cream right out of the bag. Cleanup is fast too! Serves 1.

Fall

Go on a Corn Stalk

199 A crisp autumn day practically begs for this corny contest. All you need is one ear of dried corn per player. Hide the corn around the yard in spots that are neither obvious nor too hard to find. Now round up everyone and explain that the object is for each player to retrieve an ear and remove all of its kernels (just rub them off). The first one to succeed is the winner. Once everybody in the group has accomplished the task, you can feed the kernels to the squirrels and birds.

Make a Mini Scarecrow

200 These toy sentries are just right for decorating a windowsill or autumn wreath.

MATERIALS

Corrugated cardboard

Fabric scraps

Yarn

Glue stick

Popsicle sticks

Fine-tipped pen

From cardboard, cut out individual shapes that resemble a miniature shirt, pants, and hat. Trace around each shape onto two contrasting fabric scraps (one to cover each side of the cardboard). Cut out the cloth tracings and set them aside.

For straw, snip yarn into short lengths and use a glue stick to affix several to both sides of your cardboard cutouts at the ends of the arms and legs and to the center of the hat brim. Then glue the fabric cutouts to the cardboard and atop the straw.

To assemble the scarecrow, insert a Popsicle stick through the corrugated center of the cardboard pieces (as shown at left), leaving a space between the shirt and hat for a face. Draw on eyes and a mouth with a fine-tipped pen.

Celebrate Fall

201 Relish the glory of an autumn day with one of these seasonal activities:

- Set up a row of pumpkins and try landing a hula hoop around each one.

- Visit a pick-your-own orchard, then make an apple pie.

- Iron brightly hued leaves between two sheets of waxed paper to make colorful window decorations.

- Turn your kids' outgrown clothes into a scarecrow to pose on your porch.

Pumpkin Smoothies

202 This easy-to-make treat offers a taste of pie in a glass — perfect when you're squashed for time.

In a blender, combine 1/2 cup of canned pumpkin, 3/4 cup of milk or vanilla yogurt, 1/4 teaspoon of cinnamon, 1/8 teaspoon of nutmeg, 2 teaspoons of brown sugar, and 4 ice cubes and puree until smooth. Pour the smoothies into small glasses (this drink is rich) and garnish each with a dollop of vanilla yogurt or whipped topping. For a fun touch, add a pinch of cinnamon or a few colored sprinkles. Serves 2 or 3.

FUN FACT Stand anywhere on earth with a compass in your hand, and the needle will point north. Why? Because our planet's core is magnetized. Although its pull is weak by the time it reaches the planet's surface, the magnetism is still sufficient to turn a compass's lightweight needle relatively in line with the earth's axis.

Fall Trail Mix

203 To keep your kids nourished trailside, gather some of their favorite berries and nuts and whip up a sweet and crunchy snack. In a large mixing bowl, stir together 2 cups of dry-roasted, unsalted peanuts, 2 cups of raw sunflower seeds, 1 cup of raw pumpkin seeds, 1 cup of raisins or dried sweetened cranberries, and 1 cup of mini chocolate chips. Store in an airtight container.

Stick Grip

204 Here's a way for kids to spruce up and personalize a favorite walking stick.

MATERIALS

Old T-shirt

Wooden beads

Walking stick

Tear or cut an old T-shirt into 1-inch-wide strips. Tie the strips end to end to create three strips roughly 2 yards long.

Thread a bead or two onto the end of each strip and tie a knot in the strip to hold the bead in place.

Tie all three strips together about 4 inches from the beads. Braid the strips.

Make a wrist strap with the end closest to the beads by tying off a loop big enough for a hand to fit through. Hold the loop against the walking stick and thread the other end of the braid through the middle of the loop, as shown. Pull it tight.

Tightly wrap the rest of the braid around the top 6 inches of the walking stick to form a grip. Tie off the braid by looping the end through the last few wraps.

Make a Paper Bag Head

205

Put a happy face on a plain paper bag — for handing out Halloween treats, or just for ferrying your lunch.

MATERIALS

- Colored markers
- Plain lunch-size paper bag
- White crayon or chalk
- Stapler
- Raffia

Use the markers to draw scarecrow-style facial features on the bag. Use the white crayon or chalk for eyes and teeth. Once the bag is filled — with goodies or lunch — staple the top closed and add a bundle of raffia for hair.

The Shape of Things to Fall

A tree can often be identified by the shape of its leaves. Can you make the match? (Answers below.)

 A.

 B.

 C.

 D.

 E.

 F.

1. Scarlet oak: Its leaves provide a natural litmus test — the brighter their fall coloring, the more acidic the surrounding soil.

2. Sugar maple: The amount of sugar these leaves contain determines the hue of the foliage, which ranges from deep red to orange to brilliant yellow.

3. American beech: After the leaves turn a rich yellow-bronze in fall, they often remain on the lower parts of the tree throughout the winter.

4. Quaking aspen: Its golden-yellow autumn leaves flutter in the slightest breeze.

5. Sassafras: In the fall, outer sassafras leaves turn red or orange, while inner leaves turn yellow; this makes the tree appear to glow.

6. Ginkgo: A tough survivor from the Triassic Period, it thrives even in an urban setting. Look for its gold leaves in autumn.

Answers: A-3, B-1, C-5, D-6, E-2, F-4

FUN FACT Leaves don't really change color in the fall. Rather, as daylight decreases, cells at the base of the leaves swell, cutting off the flow of fresh water and causing chlorophyll (which makes leaves look green) to disappear. Other pigments that have been there all along, such as red and orange, become visible.

1 foot along the fold and mark the spot. Then cut a 6-foot length of rope. Have your child hold one end of the rope at the marked spot while you tie the opposite end around the colored marker. Step away from your child until the line is taut and move the rope in an arc, marking a line on the canvas as you go. Cut the tarp along the line and then cut out a 12- by 6-inch rectangle to the left of the marked spot at the top corner of the tepee.

Now you're ready to assemble the tepee. Loosely tie together three of the PVC pipes 2 feet down from the tops with a piece of rope, then stand them up like a tripod. Lean the remaining poles against the tripod so that they are evenly spaced.

Drape the cut canvas around the tepee frame, overlapping the top a bit. Make two sets of holes through both layers of the overlapped portion and thread the chopsticks through them to hold the canvas in place.

 To secure the lower edge of the canvas to the frame, first snip a small hole about 1 inch in from one of the tarp's bottom corners. Loop a short length of rope through the hole, as shown, and tie the ends around the base of one pole (this pole will become part of the doorway). Now gently stretch the canvas around the PVC frame so that the canvas extends past the first pole to create a door flap. Snip a small hole near the lower edge of the canvas where it falls on the remaining poles and tie it in place using the same method as before.

Tom Thumb

206 **With** **non-**toxic ink pads, your child can make fall turkeys for Thanksgiving cards and pictures. Just use a thumb to print the turkey's body and fingertips to create a head and feathers. Use markers to add a beak, wattle, and feet.

Backyard Tepee

207 Like the Native American tepee that inspired it, this shelter can be assembled and dismantled in a jiffy. Best of all, it provides a fun play space on a sunny fall day.

MATERIALS

- **9- by 12-foot canvas tarp or drop cloth**
- **Measuring tape**
- **Colored marker**
- **White cotton rope**
- **Ten 8-foot-long white PVC pipes, 3/4 inch in diameter (an adult can cut longer PVC pipes to length with a hacksaw)**
- **2 chopsticks or similar strips of wood**

Fold the tarp in half so that it forms a 9- by 6-foot rectangle. Measure in

Paint a Fall Mural

208

Hosting a harvest dinner or Halloween party? This activity lets all the guests have a hand in painting a decorative autumn mural. All it takes is a large sheet of white or brown nonglossy wrapping paper tacked to a family room wall or outdoor fence, tempera paints, and paintbrushes.

Start by painting a big yellow-leafed maple tree in the center or fence pickets across the bottom. If your group of artists needs further inspiration, try writing the names of different symbols of fall, such as a jack-o'-lantern, a scarecrow, or a harvest moon, on slips of paper and putting them in a paper bag. Then everyone can draw slips from the bag and paint those objects into the scene.

Stamp an Apple-picking Bag

209

You can make apple prints on T-shirts, on wrapping paper, on tablecloths, on backs and bellies. Heck, you can stamp them just about anywhere. Even the youngest children can make this aptly appley sack to use on your next excursion to a pick-your-own orchard.

MATERIALS

- **Newspaper**
- **Fabric bag (cloth grocery sacks work well)**
- **Fabric paint (brown, green, and red)**
- **Paintbrush**
- **Apples**

Slip several layers of newspaper into the fabric bag so that the paint will not seep through. With a paintbrush, use brown paint to fashion a tree trunk. Let it dry. Then use a horizontally cut apple to make leaves by brushing a thin layer of green fabric paint onto the apple and pressing it around the top of the trunk. Repeat several times (make sure to look for the star in the print!). After the green paint dries, cut an apple in half vertically. Brush it with red fabric paint. Then "hang" juicy apples on the tree.

Winter

There's Snow Place Like Home

210 A cheerfully chilly snow person is a true icon of winter, and we love the warmth of our parent-child pair. Just wait for perfect snow, get out your waterproof mittens, and start sculpting.

MATERIALS

Snow	Mittens
Charcoal briquettes	Scarf
Carrots	Child's snow pants,
Apple chunks	winter boots,
Toothpicks	mittens, and
Stones and sticks	hat

Start with a three-snowball body for the parent and add charcoal briquette eyes, a carrot nose, an apple-chunk mouth (secured with toothpicks), and stone buttons. Use sticks to support mittened hands, then wrap a scarf around the neck.

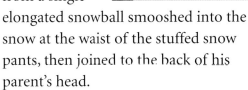

The snow child is formed from the bottom up, starting with snow pants stuffed with packed snow. His torso is a made from a single elongated snowball smooshed into the snow at the waist of the stuffed snow pants, then joined to the back of his parent's head.

Use a stick brace to support the child on his parent's shoulders, then stuff boots into his snow pants and use snow to hold his mittens in place. Form his snowy head with a point to support his hat, and make his face as you did his parent's.

Snowballs in July

"We have two children, Calley, age eight, and Cole, seven. I always make a big deal about their birthdays, inviting all their classmates to our home to celebrate. Last year, before winter ended, I made about 60 snowballs, wrapped them in plastic wrap, and put them in our freezer until our set of summer birthdays rolled around. On a hot day, snowballs can be a lot of fun! We made up several games and relays, and the snowballs made for a truly memorable party."

— *Shirley Hooey, Lakota, North Dakota*

Marshmallow Snowman

211 Here's a sweet treat that's a piece of cake to make. Start with a wedge of angel food cake and spoon on whipped cream snow. Next, push thin pretzel sticks through the center of a stack of three marshmallows to create a snowman's body. Stick two more pretzels into the sides of the stack to form arms, and press on candy bits for facial features and buttons. Tie on a fruit leather scarf and fashion a hat out of gumdrops. Then place licorice stick skis on top of the snow and use a pretzel to anchor the snowman atop the skis.

A Slick Trick

212 Here's a cool feat your child can pull off — or up. Have him challenge his friends to pick up an ice cube with a piece of string. Once they've tried (and given up), he can sprinkle some salt on the cube and lay the end of the string on the salted area. The ice will melt and then quickly re-freeze, adhering to the string, which will allow him to pick up the cube with ease.

Snow Château

213 Forget summer's plain old sand castles. Winter means your kids can construct beautiful rainbow-colored ice castles.

MATERIALS

Plastic containers (pails, gelatin molds, plastic storage containers, cups)
Food coloring

Fill the containers with water. Add food coloring (we used about 20 drops of color per cup of water) and freeze outside overnight. When you're ready to build, bring the ice to room temperature. When the ice turns in its container, that means it's ready to slip out. Voilà! Crown yourself royal architect and build away.

Color Your World

214 Got a snowy fort to decorate? Or the blank slate of a snowbank? Go ahead and paint it. We fill spray bottles with food coloring and water (about six drops per bottle) and let the troops run wild. Thinking of a more precise look? If the surface is solid and smooth, try working with regular tempera paint and paintbrushes.

Ice Light

215 This crystal lantern may be as cold as ice, but it's guaranteed to cast a warm glow. To make one, you'll need a large metal mixing bowl, a plastic yogurt container, a cupful of coins, and, of course, freezing temperatures. Start by pouring a couple of inches of water into the mixing bowl. Place it outdoors to freeze. Fill the yogurt container with stones or coins, then center it on the ice in the bowl. Slowly pour more water into the bowl, so that it nearly reaches the rim of the smaller container, and let it freeze solid. To remove the lantern from its mold, run warm water around the outside of the bowl and the ice should slip out. Dump out the contents of the inner container and pour in warm water to loosen it. Remove the container and place a votive candle in the opening.

Indoor Igloos

When it's just too chilly to go out, bring winter in. A few shovelfuls of snow in the tub will keep your kids busy till it melts. Or get out a bag of sugar cubes and a tub of frosting, and let your kids build mini igloos — good wintry fun, minus the frostbite factor.

Snowgusta National

216 Backyard golfers will enjoy the challenge of a course where the greens are always slick and the changing conditions — ice, slush, blizzards — keep the game exciting.

MATERIALS

- **Food coloring and spray bottles**
- **Assorted obstacles and plastic containers**
- **Ski poles or dowels, tape, and felt**
- **Rubber ball and hockey stick**

For a perfectly manicured green, stomp down an area around each hole (hard-packed snow holds color better than fluffy snow), mix water and green food coloring in a spray bottle, then spray the mix on the packed snow.

Once your green is set, add wacky obstacles like these: pool toy rings or a hula hoop sunk halfway in the snow, a toboggan or skateboard upside down, a trash can lid, or a tunnel through the bottom of a snowman. And don't forget to make holes. We used recycled plastic containers sunk in the snow. Top ski poles with taped-on felt flags.

It's a snow in one! Using a rubber ball and his hockey-stick nine iron, our pro sinks an ace.

It's a good thing sleds don't get speeding tickets. Fastest documented sled speed: 247.93 mph, set by Sammy Miller in 1981 on a rocket-powered sled on Lake George, New York. Fastest undocumented sled speed: 650 miles per second – set every year by Santa.

KITCHEN ART

Pasta Doodles

217 Even if it never gets cold where you live, your kids can still play in the "snow" — by turning pasta shapes into ornate flakes.

Working on waxed paper, arrange wagon wheels, bow ties, and other dried pastas into different geometric patterns. Once you've settled on a few that you like, use a toothpick dipped in glue to stick together the pieces of each one. Let the glue dry completely. Then peel away the waxed paper and hang your snowflakes from a window frame or the ceiling.

SNOW GAMES

A Flurry of Fun

218 One of the cool things about snow is that it only takes a few inches of the stuff to have a pile of fun. Try one of our favorite frosty games.

Rope Tow: Team up for a slip-sliding variation of tug-of-war. Tamp down a wide, shallow trench in the snow to serves as the midline. Then take up positions at the ends of a long, thick rope and let the tugging and towing begin.

Whichever team pulls the entire opposing group over to its side of the trench wins.

Hat Trick: Once you've built a plump snowman to stand sentry in your front yard, make a game of topping him off in style. Take turns trying to land a hat on his head by throwing it Frisbee style from about 10 feet away.

Snowballs

219 Your kids will be naturals at shaping and rolling these buttery snowball cookies. But don't expect these treats to last any longer than the real ones — they melt as soon as you pop them into your mouth.

INGREDIENTS

1	cup walnuts
1	cup margarine or butter, softened
½	cup confectioners' sugar, plus extra for rolling
1	teaspoon vanilla extract or maple syrup
2¼	cups all-purpose flour
¼	teaspoon salt

Finely chop the walnut meats in a blender or food processor, then set them aside. Cream together the margarine and the ½ cup of confectioners' sugar. Add the vanilla extract or maple syrup. Stir in the flour, salt, and nut meal.

Roll the dough into 1-inch balls and place them an inch apart on an ungreased cookie sheet. Bake in a preheated 400° oven until set but not brown (about 10 minutes).

Roll the cookies in confectioners' sugar while they're still warm and then again when they've cooled. Makes about 4 dozen.

FUN FACT Snow may look white, but the billions of tiny ice crystals that make up snow are really clear. Instead of reflecting a particular color (in the case of an apple, a shade of red), snow crystals reflect all the colors of the spectrum – a combination that appears white to the human eye.

They're Not Just a Bunch of Flakes

220 Snow is made up of strikingly beautiful crystals, falling singly or in the clumps we call flakes. See for yourself. Chill a sheet of black paper in your freezer, take it outside during the next storm, and as the flakes land, examine them with a magnifying glass. Can you find these six major crystal types? **Stellar crystals:** Look for these in a windless snowstorm (they break in rough weather). **Plates:** Is the snow sparkling? Light often reflects off these mirrorlike crystals. **Spatial dendrites:** Feathery and irregular, these crystals float down from the sky at 2 to 3½ mph. **Columns:** These dense crystals can act like small prisms, creating halos around the moon. **Capped columns:** These are also called *tsuzumi* crystals, after a similar-shaped Japanese drum. **Needles:** Although long and thin, these common crystals have six sides.

Nature T-shirt, page 161

CHAPTER SIX

Arts & Crafts

Presenting more than 50 projects to bring

out the artist in your child

OVER THE YEARS, we here at *FamilyFun* have written about thousands of crafts. As time passes, a few of them emerge as classics, members of what we call our Crafts Hall of Fame. To make it into this exclusive club of plaster beetles and aquarium-tube bracelets, a craft not only must be easy, inexpensive, and made from readily available materials, but also must have that elusive "wow" factor. It has to be so cool that when you and your kids spy it in our pages, you don't just say, "We could do that," but "We can't *wait* to do that."

Well, we've selected dozens of great crafts for this chapter, from bright ideas for dressing up your kids' clothes to simple projects that turn beach finds into keepsake treasures. And they all embody that boredom-shattering wow factor we prize. Take our geodesic dome (page 140). What makes it a classic Crafts Hall of Famer? For one thing, you can create it with just a stack of newspaper

and a stapler. For another, its ingenious design is easy, yet absorbing enough to take up the better part of a rainy day. Plus, your kids can play with (and in) it for days or weeks, and then recycle it when they're done!

As you skim through the following pages, you'll find a range of craft ideas. Some can be made quickly and easily by an unassisted child; others can busy a family for an entire afternoon. Many are crowd-pleasers — simple, mass-producible, and inexpensive enough to be created en masse by a large group of glue-stick-wielding crafters. We offer you this wealth of projects, and a few helpful tips.

Gather materials before you begin. There's nothing worse than realizing halfway through a project that you're out of tempera paint or construction paper. Read all the way through the directions and amass the necessary supplies before you start a project — or decide in advance that you'll be happy to improvise where necessary.

Beach Butterflies, page 155

Arts & Crafts

135

Trash Treasures, page 146

Emphasize the process. It's fine to have an end result in mind, but make sure you aren't so determined to follow directions that your child can't add her own flair. The end result, after all, is no more important than the steps that lead up to it. So, when you're trying a new project, always ask yourself, "Can my child be creative with what we're doing here, or am I running an assembly line?"

Encourage respect. The happiest artists have a healthy respect for themselves and their own projects, and for the artwork of their peers. Teach them to appreciate the unique quirks of each artist, and to use descriptive, nonjudgmental language with one another ("Wow! You've really used a lot of blue in that painting!"). While you're at it, it's not a bad idea to teach respect for the materials themselves, setting basic ground rules for capping pens and glue, washing out paintbrushes, and protecting surfaces and clothing.

Make cleanup part of the project. Cleaning up as you go will help preserve order in your workspace, and it may also save art supplies from an early demise. Start this habit early, and it will become a part of your child's regular craft ritual. And why not make it fun? Try putting on an upbeat song and cleaning up as much and as quickly as you can before the music ends.

The Craft Supply Closet

There is probably nothing more crucial to your child's artistic happiness and independence than having a well-stocked store of supplies. Get the best ones you can afford and keep them easily accessible. Consider keeping:

- Paper (white, construction, and a large roll of newsprint)
- Paints (tempera, watercolor, finger, and acrylic) and paintbrushes
- Scissors
- Glue (glue sticks, white glue, tacky glue, and a glue gun)
- Markers
- Crayons and colored chalk
- Pencils, colored pencils, and a sharpener
- Tape (clear, masking, and double-sided)
- Paper clips and a stapler
- Clay (modeling and polymer)
- Sewing supplies
- Recyclables (toilet paper tubes, newspaper, egg cartons, and so on)
- Fun extras like glitter, sequins, pipe cleaners, beads, craft foam, yarn, ribbons, tissue paper, and googly eyes

Paper

Collage Quilts

221 A quilt is, perhaps, the quintessential American craft, combining industry with beauty and thrift. With this paper collage activity, you can host a scaled-down version of an old-style quilting bee for your child and a pal.

To start, you'll need several sheets of colored paper, a ruler, a pencil, scissors, a 4-inch white poster board square for each child, and a glue stick. Cut the colored paper into 6- by 1-inch strips. Then cut each strip into six 1-inch squares. Next, snip most of the squares in half diagonally to create triangles.

Now your child can experiment with various quilting patterns by arranging the pieces on top of the poster board square. She can even customize her design with a larger colored shape or a border. Once she decides on a particular design, help her glue the pieces in place.

HOMEMADE NECKLACE

Paper Leis

222 A trademark of Hawaiian hospitality, leis are typically made from fragrant flowers. Our paper ones are unscented, but they make a festive birthday craft or a cheering rainy-day play activity.

MATERIALS

   Muffin pan liners

   Embroidery needle

   Yarn

To make each flower, flatten one or two muffin pan liners and trim the edge of each to create petal shapes. Then cut a round flower center from the bottom of another liner and leaves from green liners or tissue paper, if desired.

Once you have a dozen or so flowers, thread the embroidery needle with a strand of yarn long enough to form a loop that fits loosely over your child's head. String on each flower, starting with the leaves and followed by the petals and a center, spacing them evenly along the strand. Tie the yarn ends together, and you've got a pretty paper lei.

Fashion Plates

Dinner Plate Portraits

"My daughter, Amanda, age ten, enjoys making her own paper dolls from discontinued pattern books, which usually sell for $1 to $3 at fabric stores. She cuts out the figures, then glues them onto pieces of cardboard. Amanda also cuts out pictures of clothing from the books, leaving tabs at the edges to help the outfits stay on the dolls. Not only are these paper dolls inexpensive, but the pattern books offer an extensive variety of people and outfits."

— *Peggy Schulten, Elgin, Illinois*

223 Whether your kids are preschoolers or preteens, this mask-making project is a real crowd-pleaser. The kids can cut out pictures of favorite rock stars, clothing, and accessories from magazines to create plates that are part mask, part instant autobiography.

using the supplies set out to create hair, eyes, lips, noses, freckles, and other features. If your crowd isn't big enough to pair everyone up, let them make self-portraits. And be ready with some sharp scissors to make eyeholes for those artists desiring real "vision" in their portraits.

MATERIALS

Paint stirrers

Heavy-duty paper dinner plates

White glue and glue sticks

Old magazines and catalogs

Markers and crayons

Colored construction paper or card stock

Yarn and/or fun fur

Scissors

Attach a wooden paint stirrer as a handle to the bottom of each plate. To help the handle lie flat over the plate rim, cut a tab in the plate that's the same width as the stirrer. Then use white glue to attach the handle to the tab and to the back of the mask.

Set out magazines, markers, crayons, construction paper, yarn, fun fur, and other decorating supplies, along with glue sticks and scissors. Hand each child a mask and ask her to pair up with a pal. Have the paired-up kids sit face-to-face so they can do portraits of each other,

Set Up House

224 If you've got stacks of magazines and holiday catalogs hanging around, let your kids fill an afternoon, or more, with this fun and endless 2-D project.

MATERIALS

- Poster-size piece of paper
- Catalogs
- Scissors
- Glue sticks
- Paper and markers
- Clear Con-Tact paper
- Double-sided tape

For each child, draw a house shape on a poster-size piece of paper, then set out catalogs, scissors, glue sticks, paper, and markers and let the decorating begin. Each person can custom-design her own house — filling it with everything from furniture to teapots to fishbowls. Encourage kids to add fantasy touches: What would make houses more fun? Bunk beds five high? A system of pulleys and chutes? To make their creations more durable, you can help attach the "permanent" fixtures (couches, tables) to the house by covering them with Con-Tact paper. Objects that might need to be moved around (pet dogs or people) can be covered front and back with Con-Tact paper and cut out (double-sided tape on the back will help them stick in place). Still have catalogs left? Challenge your kids to make a whole town.

Mosaic Mural

226 In ancient Rome, artisans pieced together small stone squares to create exquisite floors that were both a feast for the eyes and a cool treat for the feet on days when temperatures soared. Using the same method, your child can create mosaic art of his own.

First, sketch a basic design on poster board and cut or tear colored paper into a bunch of small squares. Working in sections, apply glue to the poster board and press on paper squares, spacing them slightly apart just like a stone mosaic.

Sandpaper Bookmarks

225 Your child can dress up the books she reads with these place holders made from scratch.

To make one, first cut out two matching bookmark shapes, one from white construction paper and one from fine-grained sandpaper. Pressing down firmly, use crayons to create a design on the sandpaper. Lay the white paper squarely atop the drawing and set them both on top of several sheets of newspaper. With an iron on medium heat (adults only), iron over the white paper, then carefully lift it away (it will be hot!). When it has cooled, cover the bookmark with clear Con-Tact paper.

Build a Geodesic Dome

227 Who would ever believe that the Sunday paper and a stapler would be all you need to create a life-size structure big enough to hold a bevy of children? Black and white and fun all over, our dome is, at turns, a fort, a gingerbread house, a cave, and a camping tent. And after the fun, it is easily turned back into plain old recyclable newspaper.

MATERIALS

100 sheets of newspaper (choose a paper with large-size pages — tabloid size is too small — and use the full square spread)

Pencil

Masking tape

Yardstick

Stapler

Glue stick (optional)

Colored tissue paper (optional)

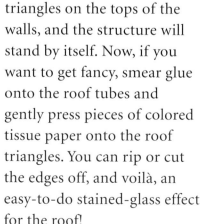

You'll need four sheets to make each newspaper log. Spread the sheets open flat, one on top of the other. Set the pencil in the corner and roll across the diagonal (see step 1, below). Use the pencil as a general guide to help you roll evenly; don't try to roll the newspaper as thin as the pencil! When you get to the other end of the paper, you'll have a tube. Slip the pencil out and tape the tube shut. Repeat this process until you have 25 tubes. Then trim the ends, using a yardstick to make sure all the tubes are the same length. Ours were each about 30 inches long.

At this point, you'll need a big, open space to construct the dome in. Staple three tubes together to create a triangle. Repeat the process until you've constructed five triangles like the one shown in step 2.

Staple the five triangles to each other at their bottom

corners. Add five connecting tubes across the top (see step 3). Then raise the triangles, or walls, off the floor and staple the ends together to form a pentagonal structure. It helps to have a few kids hold up the walls while you staple.

Take the remaining five tubes and staple their ends together at the center to make a star (see step 4). Staple the free ends of the star to the junctions of the triangles on the tops of the walls, and the structure will stand by itself. Now, if you want to get fancy, smear glue onto the roof tubes and gently press pieces of colored tissue paper onto the roof triangles. You can rip or cut the edges off, and voilà, an easy-to-do stained-glass effect for the roof!

Life-size Paper Dolls

228 This paper alter ego is easy to fashion and a blast to outfit. Just trace around your child's body on brown paper and cut out the form. Brush the entire body with a thin layer of white glue and stick it, back to back, to another piece of paper (this will keep the doll from curling up). Cut out the doubled shape and let the glue dry. Your child can use construction paper to decorate the doll and make hair. Have your child trace around the doll to fashion clothes from wrapping or construction paper, felt, or anything that strikes her fancy. Cut out the clothes and use paper clips to dress the doll in its new wardrobe.

Newspaper Sandals

229 Read all about it! Then roll it up and hit the town in these spiffy sandals, adapted from *The Anti-Boredom Book*.

MATERIALS FOR A PAIR

About 30 newspaper sheets (half of a full double-page)

Masking tape and craft glue

Roll each sheet of newspaper lengthwise into a tight tube and tape it. Press each tube hard along its length to flatten it into a 1-inch-wide strip. For each sandal, begin by making a 2-inch fold at one end of a strip and then coiling the strip tightly around the folded section. Tape the next strip to the end of the first and continue winding and taping until the oval is half the length of your foot. For a stronger sandal, wind a strip tightly across the width of the oval and tape it. Wind more strips around the outside of the sandal until it is big enough for your foot, then tightly tape around the entire perimeter (see Figure A).

For a strap, thread one end of a strip between two outer strips, then thread the other end through the other side (B). Position the strap so it fits your foot, then trim the ends and secure them with lots of glue or tape or both.

To finish the sandal, trace your foot on a colored sheet of newspaper (try the funnies!), cut out the shape, and glue it to the foot bed of the sandal. Finally, cut two 1-inch-wide strips from the same decorative newspaper and glue them around the edge and the strap of the sandal. Let dry, and strut!

A

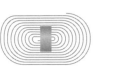

B

Paint

Swirl Postcard

230 Based on the age-old principle that oil and water don't mix, this marbleized paper is one of those projects that looks difficult but is easy enough for a six-year-old.

MATERIALS

- Tupperware container, or aluminum foil or plastic takeout containers
- Small plastic eyedroppers
- Two or more colors of enamel paint (the kind used for models)
- Toothpicks or sticks
- A pack of white watercolor postcards or index cards

Fill your container halfway with water. Using an eyedropper, add a few drops of paint in different colors to the water. Swirl the colors with a toothpick or stick. Drop a blank card on the water. After a second or two, carefully lift the card straight up and set it aside to dry on newspaper or paper towels. When it's completely dry, if the card curls, place it beneath a heavy book for a couple of days to flatten the edges. **Tip:** You may want to clear the water between card dips by dragging a toothpick through the water.

PAINTING PROJECTS

Let's Paint!

231 Nothing celebrates color like paint. Get your child into a smock, mix up one of our fun recipes, and let her color her world. **Decorate your windows** with these easy-to-clean-up hues: mix 1 part powdered tempera paint with 2 parts clear dishwashing liquid and apply with paintbrushes. The dried paint wipes away easily with a dry paper towel. Make your own **puffy paint** by mixing drops of food coloring with 1 part each of flour, salt, and water. Use a squeeze bottle to paint designs on paper, which will dry puffy and textured. **For mess-free "finger painting,"** sandwich globs of tempera paint between two sheets of waxed paper, then press and squish to swirl the colors. To make prints of the resulting designs, remove the top sheet of waxed paper and lay a piece of plain paper atop the paint.

FamilyFun BOREDOM BUSTERS

Eric Carle Collage

Spread out the newspapers. Using a large paintbrush, completely paint a piece of paper one color. Paint contrasting dots with a small paintbrush or squiggles with a medium brush. For a funky, textured look, dip one of the found objects — say, the sneaker sole — into another paint color and press it all over the paper. Continue until you have enough papers to create your collage (about ten should do). Spread out the papers to dry completely.

On scrap paper, sketch an outline of the collage you'd like to create. We've chosen a bird, but the possibilities are endless: try a sailboat, a garden of flowers, even your own version of Carle's famously lonely firefly. Using this sketch as a guide, cut out the shapes from the painted papers.

Arrange the cutouts on white paper. Using the glue stick, glue down the large central piece of the picture first. Glue down the rest of the picture around it, according to the blueprint sketch you've created. Finally, draw in finishing touches such as eyes and feet with crayons or colored pencils.

232 Nobody can transform scraps into art like Eric Carle, beloved author of *The Very Hungry Caterpillar.* But his step-by-step instructions will bring out the collage master in your child.

MATERIALS

- **Newspapers**
- **Acrylic or tempera paints and paintbrushes**
- **White paper**
- **Found objects such as a carpet scrap, an old sneaker, sponges, a plastic comb, a slice of potato cut into a star**
- **Glue stick**
- **Crayons or colored pencils**

Quick Draw

"When my sons, Justin, now age 15, and Joshua, 12, were younger, I discovered an easy way to keep them amused while waiting for our order at a restaurant or while on a trip. I would keep a small pad of paper in my handbag, and whenever we found ourselves with a few extra minutes, I would draw random squiggles or shapes on pieces of paper and let them fill in the rest. At first, I drew shapes that resembled something specific (like a fish or a turtle). As they got older, I began making the squiggles more complex and encouraged them to turn the sheets upside down and sideways to look for other possibilities. In the beginning, they just drew faces, but before long they had created spaceships, aliens, monsters — even new animal species."

— Susan Michalczak, Orlando, Florida

PLASTER PROJECT

Paint a Batch of Beetles

233 Your kids will go buggy over this open-ended project: decorating a colony of brightly colored beetles. You might want to spread out your bug making over two afternoons: one to mold the beetles and one to paint them.

MATERIALS

> 1 cup of plaster of Paris
>
> Disposable plastic spoons
>
> Acrylic or tempera paints
>   and paintbrushes

To start, mix up the plaster of Paris according to the directions on the box.

Pour the mix into disposable plastic spoons and let them dry overnight (we usually make 20 to 40 at a time and save some for later).

The next day, pop the bugs out of the spoons and have your kids paint them. An insect guide can offer some fun inspiration for colors and designs. Painting the bugs can take up the better part of a rainy afternoon, but you can also extend this project in other ways. For example, make your beetles more functional by gluing them onto magnets. Or challenge everyone to create an interesting beetle cage from any supplies around your house (toothpicks are a good jumping-off point).

QUICK ART

Mini Mouse

234 This critter sticks to glass (and peels right off), making it a fun window and mirror decoration. Just squeeze dollops of puffy paint onto waxed paper, use a toothpick to shape them into a mouse or any other design you like, then let the paint dry overnight.

Finger Paint

235

With a batch of this quick and easy paint (which keeps in airtight containers), you can turn your young artist loose on newsprint or in the bathtub at a moment's notice.

INGREDIENTS

- **2 tablespoons sugar**
- **¹⁄₃ cup cornstarch**
- **2 cups cold water**
- **¹⁄₄ cup clear dishwashing liquid**
- **Food coloring (for vibrant colors, use food coloring paste)**

Mix the sugar and cornstarch in a small pan, then slowly add the water. Cook over low heat, stirring until the mixture becomes a smooth, almost clear gel (about 5 minutes). When the mixture is cool, stir in the dishwashing liquid. Scoop equal amounts into several containers and stir in the food coloring.

This paint contains dish soap, so it dissolves in water — which makes it perfect for bathtub finger painting. (Test to be sure bright paints won't leave a residue; most come clean with a powdered cleanser.)

Sgraffito

236 In the visual arts world, sgraffito (pronounced *skra-FEE-toe*) refers to the technique of scratching through one layer of color to get to another, with striking results. To give it a try, first cover your work area with newspaper. Apply a layer of crayon (we like to use a rainbow of colors) to a piece of heavy paper, covering as much of the page as possible. Then paint over the crayon with a mixture of equal parts tempera paint (black or another dark color) and dishwashing liquid. When the paint is dry, use an empty pen or the tine of a fork to etch a line drawing into the paint, revealing the bright crayon colors underneath. **Tip:** You can also try using dark-colored finger paints or dark crayon in place of the tempera paint.

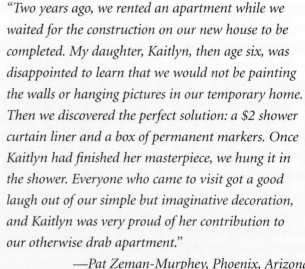

Curtain Call

"Two years ago, we rented an apartment while we waited for the construction on our new house to be completed. My daughter, Kaitlyn, then age six, was disappointed to learn that we would not be painting the walls or hanging pictures in our temporary home. Then we discovered the perfect solution: a $2 shower curtain liner and a box of permanent markers. Once Kaitlyn had finished her masterpiece, we hung it in the shower. Everyone who came to visit got a good laugh out of our simple but imaginative decoration, and Kaitlyn was very proud of her contribution to our otherwise drab apartment."

—*Pat Zeman-Murphey, Phoenix, Arizona*

Recycled Crafts

Sew Happy

"My four-year-old daughter, Tessa, and I thought it was wasteful to throw away all the colorful greeting cards she receives on her birthdays and holidays, so we created a way to recycle them: we make sewing cards. First we remove the back of the card, and then, on the front, we punch out a design using a standard hole punch. Tessa uses a darning needle and yarn (with a bit of clear tape on the end to keep it from unraveling) to weave in and out of the punched pattern. She gets to enjoy her cards again and again!"

— Terri Delzer, Bismarck, North Dakota

Trash Treasures

237 Creative crafters can make something beautiful out of even the most unlikely materials. For example:

Crushed eggshells. Parents can dye them with a mixture of food coloring paste (a dab) and rubbing alcohol (3 tablespoons); kids can glue them onto paper to make mosaics. Store the extras in ziplock bags.

Packing material. The biodegradable packing peanuts made from cornstarch can be assembled into fascinating sculptures by moistening one end of each piece with a damp cotton swab to make them stick together.

Berry baskets. Use them as weaving boards for yarn, grass, or strips of paper; cover them with construction paper for buildings; add a string handle for a carry-along treasure basket; or print with them by painting the bottoms and pressing them onto paper.

Bubble Wrap. Assuming you can stop the kids from popping it all, paint a section and use it to make polka-dot prints that look like snakeskin.

Old socks. Turn mateless socks into beanbags (cut one at the ankle, fill with beans, then sew or glue it closed) or zany puppets, like the one shown above, using whatever recyclables you have on hand.

Craft scraps. Scoop those leftover sequins, pieces of felt, and pipe cleaners into a ziplock bag. When it's full, challenge your kids to use the contents of your Rainy-day Grab Bag to make something new, such as a collage or free-form sculpture. Larger pieces of unwanted artwork can be cut into strips or squares and used to make collage cards or quilted wrapping paper.

The Paper Bag Neighborhood

238 This project illustrates two of the basic rules of boredom busting: it has a simple design that requires almost no instruction, and each child can put his own creative twist on the idea. The buildings can be purely imaginative — a fantasy house, say — or based on your actual town or neighborhood (making it a fun project for a classroom, troop, or church group).

MATERIALS

Large paper grocery bags (2 per building)

Markers and crayons

Newspaper

Glue stick and/or double-sided tape

Colored construction paper and
    poster board

Old magazines and catalogs for cutting
    out images

Toilet paper tubes

Give each child two flattened grocery bags. (If your bags have logos printed on the sides, you can create a plain surface by taping a brown paper sheet over the housefront or by carefully cutting apart the bag, turning it inside out, and taping it back together.) Have the kids decorate one of their bags with markers and crayons, drawing windows and doors, coloring in bricks or clapboards, and adding distinctive touches like cutout flower boxes and creeping ivy.

When the basic drawing and coloring are complete, stuff the second grocery bag with crumpled newspaper. Now open the decorated bag and slide it on top to create a six-sided block.

Help the crafters cut out, fold, and glue or tape in place shutters, doors, and stairs from colored paper. Add pictures of people, pets, and other images cut from magazines. Top off the house by cutting out a poster-board roof and gluing or taping it in place. For a crowning touch, add a chimney fashioned out of construction paper or a toilet paper tube.

Bottle Beings

239 They look like they're out of this world, but the fact is, you'll probably find everything you need to fashion these futuristic figures right in your recycling bin — which makes them the perfect project the next time rainy weather has your family housebound.

Fill your bottle bodies with plastic beads, pinto beans, pennies, or colored sand — anything you can pack in a plastic bottle.

For each head, use a craft knife (adults only) to cut a hole in a small ball. Make the opening just large enough to fit over the cap of the bottle body. If you're using a ball that's not hollow, such as a mini sponge ball, pull out some of the inner foam once you cut the opening (a foam football works especially well). Add facial features with acrylic paints, or use tacky glue to attach bottle cap or button eyes and milk-jug-cap ears. For hair, make holes in the ball and insert golf tees or plastic forks (trim the fork handles first).

Attach curled pipe cleaner or craft wire arms with packing tape, and tape on felt or craft foam hands.

Playful Recycling

"My daughters, Courtney and Devon, enjoy recycling interesting plastic containers into sandbox toys. Among many other treasures, we collect the tops from liquid laundry detergent bottles and other colorful lids. We also cut plastic soda bottles in two pieces, and the upper halves become funnels and the bottoms work great as sand castle molds. Our collection sits ready to grab next time we want to take a trip to the park!"

— Elaine Chenette, Midlothian, Virginia

Glitter Globes

240 These mini aquariums make great boredom busters on a day when your kids are waiting for the sun to come out.

MATERIALS

- **Baby food or jelly jar with a tight-fitting lid**
- **Polymer clay (such as Fimo)**
- **Small plastic or rubber toys and plants**
- **Water, glycerin, and glitter**
- **Small shells or aquarium gravel**

Place the jar lid on a flat surface and use a small lump of clay to stick the bottom of each plastic item to the inside of the lid. Fill the jar almost to the top with water and stir in a few drops of glycerin and ½ teaspoon of glitter. Add shells and aquarium gravel. Finally, tightly screw the lid onto the jar. Then invert the globe and enjoy the glittery show.

Bobbing Bird

241

With its comical waddle and tuxedolike coat, a penguin is always good for a laugh. Roll a ball at this toy bird, and he'll do a bouncy jig sure to put a smile on your child's face.

To make one, use a craft knife (adults only) to cut a flap in one side of a 1-liter plastic soda bottle. Place a fist-size ball of clay inside the bottle (this keeps it from toppling too easily), then pull a white athletic sock up over the bottle from the bottom. Twist a rubber band around the bottle neck to secure the sock and use the handle of a wooden spoon to tuck the sock top into the bottle. From black craft foam, cut a rectangle that wraps three quarters of the way around the bottle and extends about two thirds of the way up from the bottom. Trim the edges to resemble penguin wings and attach them to the sock with mounting tape. Next, cut out colored-foam eyes, a beak, a bow tie, and feet and tape them in place. Top off your bird with a detergent bottle–cap hat.

To make the penguin waddle, roll a rubber ball so that it knocks the bottle smartly without tipping it over.

Tin Man

242

This is our take on a popular spud-based toy: stored under his wig lid are magnetic features your child can use to create funny expressions on his tin can face.

MATERIALS

Felt or craft foam

Glue

Permanent markers

Magnetic tape

Yarn and a rubber band

Tin can, label removed

Plastic lid that fits the can

Craft knife

From the felt or foam, cut at least three different sets of eyes and ears, noses, and mouths. For details, such as teeth and eyelashes, try gluing together layered shapes or draw them on with markers. Stick magnetic tape to the back of each feature.

To make a wig, bind together a thick bunch of yarn with a rubber band. With the craft knife, cut two holes in the plastic lid (adults only). Thread the ends of the yarn up through the holes, as shown.

Milk Men

"My kids and I came up with a cute, inexpensive craft using 'chugs' (single-serving milk jugs) — we turn them into snowmen. First, we paint the lids to look like hats and add pom-poms to the tops. Then we glue buttons down the front of the white containers, attach beads and googly eyes for a face, and tie a fabric scrap around the neck for a scarf. They are so fun and easy to make that last year, my son's second grade class made them at a party and then filled them with candies to take home."

—Amy King, Roscoe, Illinois

Box Turtle

243 To make this boxy slowpoke, start with an empty gelatin box. For the head, cut a slit in the closed end and slide in the handle of a wooden ice-cream spoon. For the legs, cut two sets of slits in the skinny sides of the box and slide in two wooden craft sticks. Tape the head and legs in place

inside the box. For the tail, poke a doubled piece of pipe cleaner into the end flap, securing it inside the flap with tape.

Paint the turtle with green acrylic paint, let it dry, then sponge-paint the box with slightly darker paint. Glue tiny pom-poms and googly eyes to the head and use a marker to draw the nostrils and toes.

HOMEMADE TOY

Dolled Up

244 Although they're made of common household materials, these dolls have personalities you can't keep bottled up.

Begin by turning a cotton sock inside out and stuffing the toe into the top of a dishwashing-liquid bottle. Turn the protruding portion of the sock right side out, pulling it down over the bottle in the process.

For the doll's face and neck, fold a piece of construction paper over the bowl of a short-handled wooden spoon. Trim the paper around the sides of the bowl and partway down the handle. Wrap a rubber band around the paper at the base of the handle to hold it in place.

Cut out and glue on a paper wig and ears. Use colored markers to draw on eyes and a mouth, or cut them from magazines. Then your child can accessorize her doll with real jewelry, hair ribbons, or a scrunchy shawl.

WATER FUN

The S.S. Juice Box

245 Hot weather invariably leads to two things: piles of empty juice boxes and thoughts of water. This craft lets you combine the two, as your young ship-wrights head out to chart the depths of the backyard kiddie pool.

MATERIALS

Scrap plastic (like an old report cover or milk jug)

Permanent markers or stickers

Hole punch

Drinking straws

Scissors or craft knife

Empty juice box

Cut a rectangular sail from the scrap plastic and decorate it with markers or stickers. Punch a hole at each end and thread the straw through.

With the scissors or craft knife (a parent's job), cut a small X in the center of the empty juice box and insert the straw and sail. Float your boat in the wading pool, and blow through another straw to send it sailing.

Nature Crafts

WOODLAND CRAFT

Stick Vase

246 It's a natural fact that kids love gathering stuff outdoors. To put that stocking impulse to good use, save all their sticks for decorating this woodsy vase that even young children can make in minutes.

MATERIALS

Sticks (about ¼ inch in
    diameter)
Clippers
Empty plastic peanut
    butter jar
2 thick rubber bands
Raffia or ribbon
Glue
Pinecones (optional)

Break or snip your sticks to about an inch longer than the jar. Put two rubber bands around the jar, an inch from the top and bottom. Now begin tucking the sticks under both rubber bands, placing them as close as possible to each other. Once you've surrounded the jar with sticks, slide the rubber bands together at the jar's middle and cover them with a decorative bow. Glue on a few pinecones, then fill the vase with flowers. For kids uninterested in flower arrangements, this vessel also makes a fine pencil holder.

Mushroom Magic

To make a mushroom-spore print on paper, carefully trim the stem and lower edge of the cap of a store-bought mushroom to expose the gills. Set the cap on paper and cover it with an in-verted glass. A few hours later, lift the glass and the mush-room to reveal a dis-tinctive spore print.

Beat-a-leaf Journal

247 This project combines your kids' most primal gathering instincts with another activity they love: banging rocks. Put the finished print on the cover of a blank notebook, and your kids will have a journal for recording their outdoor adventures.

MATERIALS

- **Green leaves**
- **Wooden board**
- **Small square of muslin**
- **Thumbtacks**
- **Flat, smooth, palm-size rock or hammer**
- **Blank journal**
- **Glue**
- **Twine, ribbon, or colored paper**

After selecting a leaf or two, lay them on the board (put a piece of paper on the board first if you don't want to stain it). Place the piece of muslin on top, tacking down the fabric at the corners so it won't shift. Using the rock or ham-mer, beat the fabric carefully but with consistent, even force. Lift up the fabric, and the leaf will have left its image in green. Glue the muslin square to the front cover of the blank journal. To cover the fabric's edges, glue on a border of twine, flat ribbon, or colored paper.

Nest Guests

248
After a brief foray for pinecones, you and your child can rustle up a happy family of owls.

MATERIALS

- Pinecones
- Tacky glue
- Googly eyes
- Brown and yellow felt
- Cardboard
- Shredded paper or fine wood packing material (sometimes called excelsior, and also sold at many craft stores)

First, you'll need to collect two large pinecones for the parents and a few small ones for the owlets. (If you can't find any outdoors, you can buy them at most craft stores.) Snip off a small portion from the bottom of each large cone so that it is flat enough to stand the cone on end.

Make eyes for all of the owls by gluing googly eyes onto felt circles. Then glue the eyes to the cone. Glue on triangular felt ears and beaks as well.

For the owls' nest, cut out a cardboard circle (large enough to fit all the pinecones on). Glue on shredded paper or fine wood packing material in the shape of a nest. Allow the glue to dry. Lastly, apply glue to the bottom of each owl and carefully stick them all in place in the nest.

Pet Snake

250
Many snakes hibernate in the winter, but this colorful reptile can contentedly bask on a sunny windowsill all year. To make one, remove the bark from a small, curvy stick and have your child paint the wood with tempera or acrylic paints. For a tongue, use a pushpin to make a small hole in one end of the stick and insert a length of twisted craft wire, setting it in place with a dab of tacky glue.

Roll a Coaster

249
To make these leaf-imprinted coasters, just take a scavenging stroll outside: leaves and pine needles make lovely lasting impressions. Begin by cutting a 4-inch square cardboard template. Cover your work area with a piece of waxed paper and use a rolling pin to flatten a 2½-inch ball of self-hardening pottery clay to a ¼-inch thickness for each coaster. Arrange a pattern of leaves or pine needles atop the clay and gently press them into the clay with the rolling pin, leaving distinct but fairly shallow impressions. Remove the foliage and position the template on top of the clay. Use a butter knife to cut around the cardboard, then lift away the excess clay. Set the coasters aside to dry on a clean piece of waxed paper (this takes a day or so). Cover the dry coasters with a thin layer of matte acrylic varnish. Let it dry for 45 minutes, then accent your designs using a damp sponge and white paint. Let the paint dry thoroughly before adding a last coat of varnish.

Arts & Crafts

Memory Stones

251 This stepping-stone path offers a concrete method of preserving your most precious harvest: happy memories.

MATERIALS

12-inch-diameter cardboard building form and
   small handsaw (optional)

Spade

Small stones or gravel

Concrete mortar mix such as Quikrete (a 60-pound
   bag will yield 3 stones)

Mixing tub or bucket, hoe, and trowel

Scrap of wood

Mementos (shells, pet rocks, broken china, small toys)

Craft knife

Make the molds. For round stepping-stones, use the handsaw (adults only) to cut a 2½-inch-wide section from the building form. In the area where you'll be setting the path, dig a hole just large enough to accommodate the form and set it into the ground, firming the soil around it. Alternatively, you can create a free-form stone by digging a hole in the shape you desire, roughly 2½ inches deep. Once the mold is ready, place a 1-inch layer of small stones or gravel in the bottom.

Mix the concrete. Following the directions on the bag, combine the concrete with water in a mixing tub, stirring it with a hoe (parents only). It's ready to pour when it doesn't fall off a hoe held

nearly parallel to the ground. Use the hoe and a trowel, if necessary, to scoop the concrete into each form. Smooth the surface with a scrap of wood.

Add mementos. When your fingertip leaves a lasting impression in the mixture (usually after one to two hours), you can start customizing. Using a stick or pebbles, write your name and the date, make impressions (of your hand, a favorite toy, a prize begonia), and add your mementos. Let the stones cure for several days — covering the stones with a cloth and misting them with water several times a day for three or four days will keep them from cracking in a severe winter. Remove the cardboard forms with a craft knife (adults only).

Beach Lights

252 A day at the beach means mayonnaise jars full of salty treasures. Why not put them to beautiful use? Your kids can sift through the day's loot and festoon these sparkling candleholders. They'll be ready just in time to light at the table.

   Use tacky glue to stick assorted shells and sea glass

onto a glass votive-candleholder (these cost less than a dollar at craft stores). Allow it to dry, add a votive candle, and light! For immediate gratification (no drying time), a parent can use a hot-glue gun to affix the treasures.

Beach Butterflies

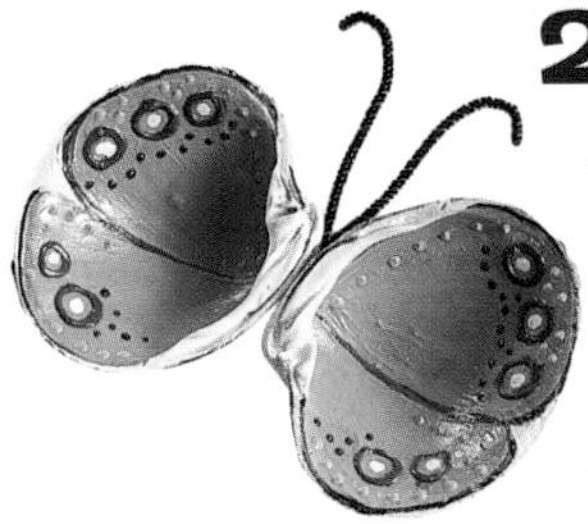

253 Before summer flies by, turn your family's beach finds into colorful keepsakes like the ones shown here. For each butterfly, you'll need a matching pair of small or medium-size clean, dry mussel, clam, or oyster shells. Arrange the pair side by side with the insides facedown and the hinged edges flush. Hot-glue the hinged edges together (a parent's job), creating a strong bond. Then bend a 6-inch length of pipe cleaner into a V and curl the tips to create antennae. Hot-glue the base of the V to the top of the glued joint. Now flip over the butterfly, and your child can use acrylic or puffy paint to adorn the insides of the shells with a distinctive wing pattern.

Chime Bracelets

254 Made with shells or lightweight trinkets, these bracelets are fun to wear because they jingle when you move.

MATERIALS

Felt

Self-adhesive Velcro fastener

Large-eyed needle and yarn

Shells or charms

Cut out a strip of felt that will fit around your child's wrist or ankle with a half-inch overlap. Stick the parts of the Velcro fastener to the ends.

With the needle, individually thread short lengths of yarn through the felt along the lower edge and knot the tops to keep them from slipping back through. Glue shells or other charms to the strands, as shown.

Nature Bingo

255 Try out this homemade beach-themed matching game. Trim index cards to fit inside a small metal box with a hinged lid (we used Altoids boxes). Use a ruler and pencil to mark each card into nine equal squares. Inside each square, use crayons or colored pencils to draw and label common nature sights, consulting a field guide as needed: we've chosen tide pools for a topic, but you could use any theme.

Put the finished cards inside the box, along with nine small, round magnets. Each player selects a card and places it inside the lid of the open tin. Every time you see a creature or plant from your card, mark it with a magnet. Three in a row — horizontal, vertical, or diagonal — wins. Or play to fill the whole card.

Ready to Wear

EASY CRAFT

Tie-dye a T-shirt

256 We love the bright hipness of these classic beauties — single-color tie-dyed T's with a circle pattern. Want to throw a summer of love party? Get out your fringed vest, put on some groovy tunes, and do your dyeing alfresco.

MATERIALS

T-shirt, washed and dried

Nickels, dimes, and quarters

Rubber bands

Fabric dye

Salt

Dishwashing liquid

EQUIPMENT

Large trash bag, cut down the middle, or a tarp
   or old shower curtain

Rubber gloves

Nonreactive metal or plastic bucket

Long-handled metal spoon

Old towel

First, prepare your T-shirt. For each circle, press a coin to the inside of the shirt, stretch the fabric tightly around it, and secure it with a rubber band (for concentric circles, bind with another rubber band or two farther along the gathered fabric).

Prepare your work area by laying the trash bag or tarp down on the ground. Put on the rubber gloves. Now mix the dye according to the package directions to make a very strong dye bath (we used ½ bottle of RIT liquid dye stirred into 1½ gallons of very hot tap water with ½ cup salt). Place your T-shirt into the bucket of dye and stir with the spoon to soak it evenly with dye. For a

dark, rich color, keep the T-shirt immersed in the dye for 20 to 30 minutes, stirring occasionally. Do not crowd the bucket.

When the shirt is dyed to your liking, remove it from the bucket and rinse it under cold running water, squeezing it, until the water runs clear.

Use scissors to snip off the rubber bands, then rinse the shirt again until the water runs clear. Finally, rinse the shirt in the bucket in warm water with a tiny squirt of dish liquid until the water runs clear. Squeeze out excess water by rolling the shirt in an old towel, then machine or hang dry.

Sleepytime Slippers

257 To make a pair of jungle slippers, place flip-flops on the back of a piece of fake fur and trace around the bottoms. Cut out the shapes, then make three slits where the foot straps join the insoles. Cover each insole with double-sided cloth carpet tape and roll the fur cutout onto the insole, adjusting it around the toe straps. Firmly press down on the fur, and slip on your slippers!

Psychedelic Tie-dye Shoelaces

258 This colorful project is sure to be a shoe-in with your kids! Just tie knots in white shoelaces about 1 1/2 inches apart. Now prepare each color of dye in its own bowl by mixing equal parts fabric paint (we used Scribblers brand) and water (we started with a tablespoon of each). If needed, add a few drops of paint (to deepen) or water (to lighten) the color. Mix with a paintbrush or stick. Dip each

knot or loop into a different color. Remove the lace from the dye after a few seconds unless you want a very dark color. Keep in mind that the colors will bleed slightly. Dry the laces flat on a plastic bag. Undo the knots when the laces are dry.

Arts & Crafts

Designer Flip-flops

259 Here's a fun project that will have your kids stepping out in the latest fashions.

MATERIALS

   Cloth ribbon, fringe, or
      similar trim
   Flip-flops with foam soles and
      foam or fabric straps
   Low-temperature glue gun

Cut a length of trim to fit around each flip-flop sole with a half-inch overlap. Cut separate pieces of trim for the left and right sides of the foot strap. To attach the trim to the sole, evenly apply a line of hot glue to a 2-inch section of the foam, using the glue gun tip to spread it if necessary. Firmly press the end of the trim onto the glued portion so that it sticks well, then smooth it toward the unglued section. Continue gluing and pressing until you've fully circled the sole. Use the same method to attach the strap trim. Dry for 1 hour.

For a matching summer hat, you can attach trim with a nontoxic fabric glue.

Friendly Face T-shirts

260

Perfect for a birthday party, sports team event, or family reunion, this project lets guests create their own favor — wearable mementos featuring the names and faces of their friends.

MATERIALS

- Prewashed cotton or cotton-mix T-shirts (one for each person)
- Sheets of cardboard
- Potato and knife
- Fabric paints
- Stiff paper plates
- Fabric paint tubes and markers

Before the party, prepare the shirts for decorating by stamping blank faces on them with your child. Begin by inserting a piece of cardboard inside each shirt. Chop a potato in half (adults only) to create an oval or circular stamp. Spread thin layers of fabric paint onto the plates and press in the potato stamp. Test the stamp on newspaper first, then on each shirt have your child stamp as many ovals as you'll have guests. Let the paint dry. At the party, set out the prestamped shirts (with the cardboard inserts still inside),

paint tubes, and markers. Guests can move from one shirt to the next, using the supplies to create a self-portrait on one of the faces and to autograph it beneath. Let the paint dry and heat-set according to the package directions.

Fleece Hat

261 This cozy cap is just the thing to keep your child's noggin warm in brisk winter weather. In fact, it's so easy to put together — there's just one seam — she could even fashion some for chilly-headed siblings and friends!

MATERIALS

Tape measure

½ yard fleece fabric

Needle and thread

Buttons, appliqués, or felt pieces for decoration

1 yard decorative cord

First, determine the size of the hat by measuring around your child's head with a tape measure. Now cut a piece of fleece that's 16 inches wide and as long as the measurement you took plus 2 inches.

Fold the fleece in half, right side in, so the 16-inch edges match up. Sew a ½-inch-wide seam along this edge, stopping 5 inches from the bottom (see Figure A). Just below the last stitch, make a ½-inch cut in from the side. Turn the material right side out. Now sew a seam along the last 5 inches of unsewn fleece (B).

Roll the bottom of the hat up two turns, so the cuff conceals the bottom part of the seam. To keep the cuff from unrolling, sew on a decorative button, an appliqué, or a felt cutout.

Finally, gather the top 3 inches of the hat and tie a colorful cord around it.

Glad Hatters

262 These decorated hats give new meaning to the expression "wearing a grin from ear to ear." All it takes to make one is a flat-top cotton hat, cardboard, fabric paints, and paintbrushes.

Start by trimming the cardboard to fit into the top of the hat; this will keep the fabric flat while you decorate it. Then paint the hat top to create a colored face (it's a good idea to mix whatever tint you choose with a bit of white to make the paint more opaque). Use two coats if needed, allowing the paint to dry after each application.

Next, lightly pencil on facial features and use different shades of paint to fill them in. Some features may need to be done in layers. To create a toothy grin, for example, first paint on white teeth only. When they dry, you can outline them with thin black lines or enclose them in bright pink lips. Once the last layer of paint dries, remove the cardboard from the hat, and it's ready to wear.

Felt fashion: For a quick decorating alternative, cut eyes, a nose, and a mouth out of adhesive-backed felt and firmly press them onto the hat.

FAMILYFUN READER IDEA

A Crafty Community

"Last summer, a group of eight parents and up to 18 kids (ages three to 16) in our small community organized and participated in a weeklong craft 'camp.' We met for three hours each morning for a week, and each day, a parent or two volunteered to teach a craft. We made tie-dyed T-shirts, batik potpourri pillows, sand candles, papier-mâché animals, garden stepping-stones, and hats from gift wrap, to name a few highlights. The kids even learned from one of the dads how to make tinware lanterns. The camp was affordable too, averaging less than one dollar per day per child to cover craft materials. We kept costs down by sharing basic supplies (glue, paints, craft sticks, and the like) and by gathering donations from a few area businesses. Our craft camp was great fun and a huge success."

— *Lucy Hardy, Wells, Maine*

CREATIVE CRAFT

Paper Bag Hats

263

Go shopping for a hat — at the grocery store! With this wacky group activity, kids can create fashion in a bag.

MATERIALS

- **Paper bags, standard grocery size or slightly smaller**
- **Tape (double-sided and clear)**
- **Pom-poms, googly eyes, pipe cleaners, feathers, and other craft supplies**
- **Construction paper**
- **Hole punch**
- **Green curling ribbon**

Help each child gently roll down the top of a bag until it reaches the size hat he wants to wear. Have him try it on for size; if it slips over his eyes, pinch the brim to adjust the size, then tape.

Now set out craft materials for decorating the hat. Kids can make their hats as simple or as elaborate as they like. They can use double-sided tape to attach pompoms, googly eyes, and feathers. For antennae, coil a pipe cleaner around a pencil, then tape on large pom-poms. Poke the end of the pipe cleaner through the hat and tape the inside to secure.

To make a flower, cut a flower shape out of construction paper. Punch two holes in its center and thread a 3-foot-long piece of green curling ribbon through the holes. Use scissors to curl the ribbon, then stick the flower to the hat with a piece of double-sided tape.

Artful T's

264 This fuss-free fabric-stenciling technique gets your kids dressed to a T in no time.

MATERIALS

- **Con-Tact paper**
- **Craft knife**
- **Cotton or cotton-blend T-shirts**
- **Newspaper**
- **Fabric paint, paper plates, and sponges**

To get started, cut Con-Tact paper into 6-inch-wide squares or circles and let the kids pencil shapes, such as stars, zigzags, or even letters, on the backs. Then turn their designs into stencils by cutting along the pencil lines with a craft knife (a parent's job) and discarding the cutout portions.

Lay your T-shirts flat and insert a thick layer of newspaper between the front and back of each one (to keep the fabric paint from bleeding through). Peel the backs from the stencils and press the Con-Tact paper onto the shirts.

Pour several colors of fabric paint onto paper plates. Now the kids can dip sponges into the paint and blot color onto the fabric in the center of each stencil. Peel off the stencils when the paint has set for a while but before it dries.

Once the paint is dry, heat-set it according to the package directions.

Nature T-shirt

265 This method of capturing the shapes of natural objects works best with shirts in bright hues of pink, blue, and green. Lay a solid-color shirt outdoors on a hard, flat surface, such as cement, away from anything that might be damaged by bleach. Arrange leaves, flowers, and other objects in a simple design on the shirt. Only the silhouettes will show, so objects with distinctive shapes work best. If there's a breeze, set stones on the objects to hold them in place. Wearing rubber gloves, use a spray bottle to spray the shirt lightly with bleach around all the edges of the design (adults only). Let the shirt set until you see the color start to change, about a minute or so. Carefully remove and dispose of the flowers and leaves. Submerge the shirt in a bucket of water and thoroughly rinse it. Put it through the washer and dryer, and it's ready to wear. **Note:** Be sure to label the spray bottle or empty and rinse it immediately.

Arts & Crafts

BEAD CRAFT

Crystal Clear

266 It only takes a handful of translucent beads and some fishing line to make a necklace that's sure to reel in compliments.

MATERIALS

Monofilament or fishing line

Translucent glass or
plastic beads

2 clamshell bead tips

Needle-nose pliers

Barrel clasp

Start with a piece of monofilament or fishing line that's twice the desired length of your necklace. String a bead onto the line, then loop the line back around and through the bead, as shown at right (this keeps the bead in place). Using the same method, add on the remaining beads, spacing them evenly. Insert each monofilament end into a clamshell bead tip and double-knot the line to keep the bead tips from slipping off. Use the pliers to pinch the bead tips, then attach the barrel clasp.

Hand Painted

267 Here's a handful of designs to inspire your young manicurist.

Starry Nights: Top a dark undercoat with a glittery gold star.

Tiger Stripes: Apply orange polish, then top with irregular black stripes.

Checkerboard: Apply a red base coat, then add staggered rows of black squares.

Cow: Paint the nail white. Top with black patches.

Pot of Gold: Paint a mini rainbow at the tip of the nail.

HOMEMADE GIFT

Hydro Bracelets

268 *Hydro* means water, and that's just what makes the beads and glitter in these bracelets float and sparkle.

MATERIALS

- 2 feet of clear plastic tubing with a ¼-inch inner diameter and 3 inches of clear plastic tubing with a ⅜-inch inner diameter (sold in most hardware stores)
- Ruler
- Tiny beads or glitter and water

To create each bracelet (these materials make three), cut an 8-inch-long piece from the ¼-inch tubing and a 1-inch length from the ⅜-inch tubing (for a fastener). Slide both ends of the 8-inch tube into the fastener, as shown, and have your child try on the bracelet for fit. If it's too big, take it apart and trim it to size, remembering that it will need to slip over her hand. Remove one end of the bracelet from the fastener. Use a finger to stopper one end and drop in tiny beads or pieces of glitter. Now slowly fill the tube with water, leaving several inches of air so it has room to move. Carefully slide the free end into the fastener as far as it will go.

CLUTTER BUSTER

Cancan Girl

269 Although she looks like she's ready to kick up her heels, this gal is perfectly content to sit still and keep your child's stuff organized. Begin with a clean, empty can (for safety, cover the cut edge with tape). Glue pink paper around the outside of the can and create a skirt by gluing two lengths of crepe paper streamer around the can, one above the other, gathering and gluing a few inches at a time. Add a pipe cleaner waistband. Now glue on a pipe cleaner and feather headdress, hair made from strips of construction paper (curl it around a toothpick first), felt arms and hands (add pipe cleaner jewelry and fabric paint nails), and purple felt legs (use black fabric paint to create shoes and fishnet stockings). Finally, add facial features such as googly eyes, paper cheeks and lips, and curled paper lashes.

Chain Gang

270

Turn a piece of hardware into a wearable treasure. All your child will need to make this locket is a 1- by 1½-inch brass hinge, 18 inches of ball chain with a fastener, a piece of soft wire (all available at hardware stores), and two photos.

Trim two snapshots or school pictures so the faces fit on the plates of the hinge. Next, use a hot-glue gun (adults only) to fix the photos to the inner plates. To decorate, your child can glue a piece of personal artwork onto the face of the locket. Now run the wire through the top of the hinge and wrap it securely around the chain.

Puzzle Jewelry

"Don't throw away your old puzzle pieces — our family has discovered they are great for making homemade earrings and pins. For earrings, take two puzzle pieces, squirt glue on the back of each, then let the children decorate them with glitter, beads, sequins, or anything they would like. Then use hot glue (parents only) to attach a pierced or clip-on earring backing. To make pins, decorate a big puzzle piece (or glue together two smaller ones) and attach a pinback. These puzzle jewelry creations are easy to assemble and make wonderful gifts."

— *Kim Novato, Pompano Beach, Florida*

FUN FACT During the course of a typical year of Mardi Gras festivities, more than five million strands of colorful plastic beads are thrown to the crowds from dozens of parade floats.

Clip-on Jewelry

271

This flowery necklace, fashioned from paper clips and colorful garden-catalog photos, makes a great accessory for jazzing up your child's wardrobe.

MATERIALS

26 paper clips

Seed catalogs, magazines, or gift wrap

Tissue paper

Glue

Begin by connecting the paper clips into a circular chain. Then cut 26 glossy 1-inch squares from the catalogs, magazines, or gift wrap. Finally, wrap a paper square around the center of each paper clip and secure the edge with glue. For another interesting effect, try wrapping squares of gold (or another solid color) gift wrap around striped plastic-coated paper clips.

It's a Wrap

273 Here's a way for your kid to show off that lucky pebble or one-of-a-kind beach find.

MATERIALS

- 20-gauge silver-colored or copper wire
- Special stone, beach glass, shell, or other small treasure
- Leather cording
- Lanyard hook (sold at most craft stores)

Cut two 10-inch lengths of wire. Wrap the midsection of one wire around the chosen treasure and tightly twist together the ends. Likewise, attach the second wire from the opposite side, just below the first one. Bend the twisted wire pairs up alongside the treasure and join them together at the top with a few more twists. Next, form a small loop to thread the cording through. Wrap at least ¼ inch of wire around the base of the loop, then snip off the excess. Finally, cut the leather cording to the desired length plus 2 inches. Tie a lanyard hook onto one end and tie the other end into a loop.

Word for Word

272 What's your child's favorite band? What does she think is cool? Does she have a favorite expression? Now she can tell the world with this easy-to-update charm necklace made from recyclables.

Cut out a bunch of interesting words from old magazines and use a glue stick to affix them to colored plastic lids (coffee can lids work well), leaving enough space around each to create a colorful margin. Now cut out the plastic-backed words, leaving room at one end to punch a hole later, and seal each of them with clear packing tape. Trim any excess tape from the edges. Punch a hole in the plastic and attach a key ring. Finally, string all of the words onto a necklace-length ball chain.

Arts & Crafts

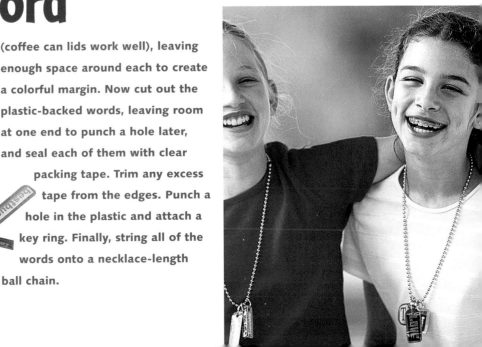

CHAPTER SEVEN

Kitchen Projects

Irresistible concoctions that your young chefs will devour

IN THE MAD RUSH to get meals on the table, we parents sometimes forget what a joyous activity cooking can be. Its pleasures are not lost on our children, who immediately appreciate the process of transforming ingredients. Through kitchen alchemy, humble foods become delicious meals or edible works of art.

Consider, for example, the pizza: bread, sauce, cheese. With some kitchen wizardry and a few toppings, these three ingredients become a kid's favorite meal. The secret to its success? Pizza, the ultimate finger food, is tasty, nutritious, and versatile. Plus, it's an absolute blast to make and decorate — the symbol, for kids, of a good time.

In the pages that follow, we've tried to adapt the selling points of this culinary all-star to a variety of recipes. You'll find ideas for every meal, snack, and celebration, and each one is easy, heartily kid approved, and fun — something to do as well as something to eat.

So capitalize on your child's curiosity and invite him or her into the kitchen.

In sharing this unhurried time together, you're sure to cook up a great appreciation of food and even, perhaps, a craving to help out with dinner. To that end:

Create a space for little chefs. Set a low table with two chairs in a corner of your kitchen. Or, if you don't have the space for this, keep a stool at the counter. Reserve a low drawer and stock it with kid-size tools: a mini rolling pin, a whisk, plastic knives, an apron, and favorite cookie cutters are good starters. We also like to keep a cooking-project shelf to inspire young bakers; ours holds a box of brownie mix, the makings for chocolate chip cookies, and some decorative basics like sprinkles, frosting, nuts, and raisins.

Set up some ground rules. You want your kids to have fun in the kitchen, but it's important to teach them safe cooking habits from the get-go. Basic rules might include hand washing, wearing an apron, tying back long hair, asking for help with the stove, and cleaning up as you go. You

Pajama Party Kids Cupcakes, page 186

may even want to post a chart in the kitchen with some reminders.

Involve your kids in your cooking projects. Whether you're making breakfast or packing school lunch, let the kids help. They can rinse canned beans in a colander for chili or, using a plastic knife, slice bananas for a fruit salad and cut up veggies to stir-fry. You may well cultivate a lifelong love of cooking. And remember: if kids have a hand in making the meal, they will be more inclined to eat it.

Egg in a
Nest,
page 171

Invite your kids to play with their food. Let them turn sliced vegetables into the flowers on page 172 before they devour them with dressing. Put half a pear on a plate and give them a pile of sprouts, pretzels, nuts, and raisins for decorating a delicious face. You supply the edible art materials, then let your kids supply the humor, the imagination, and the healthy appetites.

Make food an adventure. Get kids as close as you can to the source of the food they eat, and they're sure to learn a lot and have a wonderful time in the process. Let them bake bread from scratch — see page 181 — or make the peanut butter on page 176. Grow a vegetable garden or visit a local pick-your-own farm. See if you can get a behind-the-scenes tour of your neighborhood bakery. Or just take your kids grocery shopping with you.

Kitchen Classics

The kitchen is home to some of our favorite tried-and-true boredom busters. Here's a handful:

Get out the cookie cutters. Use them to make decorative sandwiches, fun breakfast breads, silly veggies, and, of course, cookies.

Pull down a box of pasta. It's not only the quickest, most versatile meal, it also doubles as a craft material. Make jewelry from cool shapes, or cook up a batch of spaghetti and use it to doodle on black paper.

Spend an afternoon decorating. Bake a cake, gather some fun supplies, and see what your kids come up with. Can you make a candy mosaic? Can you re-create a favorite work of art in gel frosting?

Set up a salad bar. Re-create a favorite restaurant with help-yourself bowls of colorful veggies and fun toppings.

Pretzel Log Cabin,
page 180

Breakfast Fun

Banana Smoothies

274 Start off your Saturday morning with a scrumptious and nutritious breakfast project: mixing up smoothies for the whole family. The key ingredient is a frozen banana (when your bananas get over-ripe, just peel them and store them in a bag in the freezer).

INGREDIENTS

- 1 frozen banana
- ½ cup nonfat yogurt
- ½ cup fresh orange juice
- ¼ cup blueberries, washed

Have your child measure and combine all the ingredients in a blender. Blend until smooth. Pour into a tall glass and serve with a bendy straw. Serves 1.

Funny Fruit Faces

275 Delicious and full of nutrients, fruit should be a staple of every family's breakfast menu. One way to get kids interested in new varieties is to turn tasting into an art form. Choose interesting or colorful fruits at the store or farmers market. At home, prepare the fruit and set it out buffet style, then turn the kids loose to make imaginative faces on a solid-color plate. Odds are, they'll snack as they create — and like what they taste.

FUN FACT The average American eats more than 28 pounds of bananas a year!

Pose a Puzzling Question

276 Here's a new use for that chalkboard many of us already have hanging in the kitchen. Use it to pose thought-provoking questions at the breakfast table, such as "How many zeros does a billion have?" Give a small prize to whoever thinks of the correct answer (getting to choose the night's dinner or the next family video) or challenge your kids to come up with a grown-up–stumping question.

Kitchen Projects

Bus Stop Bagel Bash

277 **Cheer your** kids with a breakfast party on the first day of school — right at your neighborhood bus stop. Call local families and ask everyone to come a half hour early and to bring a bagel topping. You provide the bagels, paper plates, and plastic knives, and if you really want to kindle some smiles, a thermos full of coffee for the grown-ups.

Bagel Portraits

278 This breakfast self-portrait may be cheesy (cream, that is), but it's a whole lot of fun — and delicious to boot!

INGREDIENTS

- Bagels (regular and mini size)
- Cream cheese
- Assorted toppings (we used lox, black olives, parsley, red and green peppers, carrots, chives, peanuts, and tomatoes)

To prepare these edible masterpieces, begin with half a bagel covered with plain or flavored cream cheese (you can use a regular-size bagel for Mom and Dad and mini-size ones for the kids). Next, create your own and your children's likenesses with anything from blueberries and chocolate chips to tomatoes and chives. Here's what we used.

Mom: Lox hair, black olive eyes, parsley eyelashes, red pepper lips, carrot nose.

Girl: Carrot hair, chive hair ribbon, green pepper eyes, chopped peanut freckles, grape tomato mouth.

Boy: Chive hair, carrot and black olive eyes, tomato mouth.

Egg in a Nest

279

Instead of serving an egg on toast, try serving it *in* toast. This breakfast classic is also known as Egg in a Saddle, Egyptian Egg, and One Eye.

INGREDIENTS

- 1 egg
- 1 slice bread
- 1 tablespoon butter

Break the egg into a bowl or ramekin. Pick out any shell fragments and set the egg aside.

Using a 3-inch cookie cutter (circle, heart, star, or flower), cut a shape out of the piece of bread.

Melt the butter in a frying pan over medium heat. Place the bread in the pan and fry it lightly on one side (you can also fry the cutout shape). Flip over the bread. Reduce the heat to low.

Have your child carefully pour the egg into the cutout hole in the middle of the bread. Cover the pan and cook for 2 to 3 minutes or until the egg has set in the bread "nest." For an over-easy egg, your child can flip the egg and bread and cook it on the other side. Serves 1.

FUN FACTS

Hens across the country collectively lay about 5.5 billion eggs each year. And what's the difference between the brown and the white eggs? On the inside, nothing. The shell color varies with the breed of hen.

Good-morning Parfait

280

Looking for a fun breakfast-in-bed recipe? Try this nutritious parfait that's quick and easy to prepare but still tastes like a decadent treat. Just fill a parfait glass with alternating layers of yogurt, granola, and your favorite sliced berries or other fruits. Dig in with a long-handled spoon!

Snack Attack

Vegetable Flowers With Homemade Ranch Dip

281 Starving kids just home from school need a snack that is wholesome, delicious, and fun too. Let them play with their food by making this creative crudité. Once their flower is in bloom, they can dip the petals in our easy-to-mix ranch dip.

INGREDIENTS

Assorted vegetables, such as radish slices, fresh spinach leaves, cucumber rounds, cherry tomatoes, celery sticks, and baby carrots

Ranch Dip

- 1/4 cup mayonnaise
- 3/4 cup buttermilk
- 2 teaspoons cider vinegar
- 1/4 teaspoon salt
- 1 teaspoon onion powder
- 1/2 teaspoon garlic powder

Set out assorted vegetables and let your kids design their own flowers. Here, we used radish slices and cucumber rounds for petals, a cherry tomato for the flower center, celery sticks for stems, and spinach for leaves.

To make the ranch dip, place all the ingredients in a medium-size bowl. Mix well with a whisk. Eat it right away with the vegetable flowers, or refrigerate it in a covered container until you are ready to use it. Makes 1 cup.

Peanut Butter Protein Balls

282 Get your kids to roll the mixture, and you can make a batch of these high-protein snacks in no time. The secret ingredient is the graham cracker coating, which complements the sweet, sticky inside.

INGREDIENTS

- **1 cup peanut butter (creamy or crunchy)**
- **½ cup nonfat dry milk powder**
- **½ cup raisins**
- **¼ cup honey**
- **Graham cracker crumbs**

In a large bowl, mix all the ingredients except the graham cracker crumbs. Shape the mixture into 1-inch balls. Roll them in the crumbs and refrigerate. Makes 24.

Stuff an Apple

283 That apple a day can be full of surprises. To make a nutritious treat, core an apple, fill it with peanut butter, and top it with raisins. The filling keeps the apple from turning brown, even when you pack it to go (transport it in a plastic bag sealed with a twist tie).

Empty Your Cupboard and Mix Up a Snack

Bite-size cereal, dried fruit, pretzels, nuts, crackers, shredded coconut — anything goes when you're tossing together a homemade snack mix, says Lori Murray of Columbus, Ohio. Lori also throws in M&M's or chocolate chips "if I'm in a good mood," she says, and mixes it all in a ziplock bag. Daughter Caitlin, age twelve, enjoys devising her own concoctions, while son Billy, seven, likes the shaking the best.

Kitchen Projects

Host a Tea Party

284 For a younger child, a tea party is an opportunity to dress up in fancy clothes, pour "tea" for friends and teddy bears, and pretend to be a fancy grown-up. It's also a grand occasion for snacking: fill the teapot with juice or herb tea and set out a small tray of finger sandwiches (cucumber and butter is a classic English teatime fave, but peanut butter and jelly or chicken salad makes a nice American substitute). Sweet treats might include a plate of special cookies, a frozen delight (see Banana Scream, below), and a bouquet of Lollipop Flowers (see page 94).

FROZEN TREAT

Banana Scream

285 This banana shake makes a frosty tea party treat. It's so thick, you'll want to serve it with a spoon instead of a straw.

INGREDIENTS

- 3 bananas (the riper the sweeter)
- 2 tablespoons nonfat milk

Peel the bananas, cut them in half widthwise, wrap in plastic wrap, and freeze until firm. Place the frozen bananas in a blender, add the milk, and puree until blended and creamy. Serve in small paper cups with small plastic spoons. Serves 4.

QUICK CRAFT

Fancy Fans

286 Perfect props for tea party guests, these lacy paper fans are a breeze to make. Use a glue stick to affix a paper doily to a sheet of colored paper, fold the sheet accordion style, then pinch together one end and secure it with a rubber band.

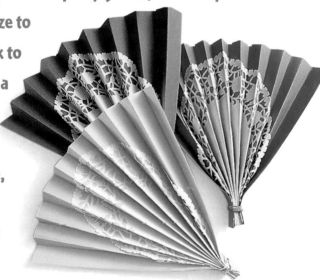

Toast Toppers

287 Snacking doesn't get any easier than toast. Toast a slice of bread, then spread it with butter, cream cheese, peanut butter, or soft cheese. Give the kids a selection of toppings – such as herbs, seeds, bread crumbs, chopped nuts, crunchy cereal, or cinnamon – that they can sprinkle over or press into the spread to create designs or faces.

Fruit-and-cheese Kabobs

288 Here's further evidence that everything has more kid appeal when it is stuck on a stick. These delightfully simple kabobs can help satisfy a craving for sweets while providing good nutritional value (protein, vitamins, and fiber).

INGREDIENTS

Apple

Cheddar cheese

Raisins

Cut the apple and cheese into small cubes. Have a handful of raisins and a few toothpicks ready.

Let your kids make tiny apple, cheese, and raisin arrangements on the toothpicks in any order they like. (You can also use pineapple, strawberries, or pears.) Eat the kabobs soon after you make them, so they're nice and fresh.

Finger Foods

289 Here are two snacks that kids can make — and then eat — with their hands. **Peanut Butter Pinwheels:** Tired of peanut butter and jelly? Spread creamy or chunky peanut butter and a little bit of honey on a fresh flour tortilla. Sprinkle with granola, roll up the tortilla, then slice it into bite-size pinwheels. **Cookie-cutter Cheese Toasts:** Kids like these because they look like cookies. Heat the oven to 350°. Place two bread slices on a cookie sheet and top each with a slice of cheese. Cut out shapes using cookie cutters, keeping the scraps for snacks. Place the cookie sheet in the oven and heat until the cheese melts.

Lunchtime

My Own Peanut Butter

For a nutty activity, help your child mix this peanut butter recipe — enough for dozens of sandwiches. Pour 2 cups of un-salted, dry-roasted peanuts into the bowl of a food processor. Process until they are finely chopped. Add 3 to 4 tablespoons of vegetable oil, processing until the peanut butter begins to form a ball. Add 1/4 teaspoon of salt and process until well combined. Transfer to a clean jar with a lid. Store in the fridge for up to two weeks. If the peanut butter separates, stir it before using. Makes 1 cup.

HEALTHY TREAT

PB & J Pizza

290 For a quick and fun-to-make lunch — perfect for a rainy day or to jazz up a back-to-school lunch box — invite your kids to assemble this no-cook "pizza." Like its cheesy cousin, this one can be customized with favorite toppings.

INGREDIENTS

3   tablespoons peanut butter
    (creamy or crunchy)

1   whole pita bread
    (medium-size)

    Toppings, such as jelly, raisins,
    grated apples, sliced
    bananas, Cheerios, and
    peanuts

Spread the peanut butter "sauce" on the pita bread. Then let your child top his pizza with favorite PB com-bos — jelly, raisins, Cheerios, grated apples, banana slices, and/or peanuts. He can arrange the toppings ran-domly or in a pattern. Use a pizza cutter to slice the pizza into wedges. Serve with a tall glass of milk. Serves 1 to 2.

Craft a Lunch Sack

291 These cheerful lunch sacks have one big advantage over the store-bought kind: they're easy to keep clean (just toss them in with the laundry!). Meredith Jack of Colorado Springs created the pattern: cut a foot-long section from a pant leg, fold over a $1/2$-inch strip around the top, and sew it down to create a casing. Leave an opening in the casing and thread through a 3-foot length of cord. For the bottom, cut another piece of fabric from the pants, about $1/2$ inch larger than the leg's circumference. Turn the leg inside out and sew the two pieces together.

Star-studded Sandwiches

292 There's no doubt that PB & J has star status among kids. Our version encourages them to dress up the classic sandwich by punching star shapes out of the bread. You can use this same method for any kind of sandwich — turkey, ham and cheese, or your child's favorite.

INGREDIENTS

- **2 slices white bread**
- **2 slices whole wheat bread**
- **Peanut butter**
- **Jelly**
- **1$1/2$-inch star cookie cutter**

Using the star cookie cutter (available at party supply stores), cut two stars out of a slice of the white bread and two stars out of a slice of the whole wheat bread. Then fit the whole wheat stars into the star-shaped holes in the white bread and the white stars into the whole wheat bread.

Now the bread is ready for the peanut butter and jelly. Have your child use a table knife to smoothly spread on peanut butter and jelly, working slowly to avoid tearing the bread. Assemble the sandwich, then wrap in plastic. Makes 2 star-studded sandwiches.

Theme Lunches

Turn your lunch into an adventure with a playful menu.

Cowboy cookout: Sloppy joes, root beer, and trail mix.

Ocean voyage: Tuna sandwiches, Goldfish crackers, and gummy sharks.

Mini meal: Mini pizzas, tiny cups of punch, and M&M's Minis.

Circus food: Hot dogs, popcorn or peanuts, and circus peanuts.

Roundabout: Bagel sandwiches, carrot rounds, and oranges.

Lunch Guests

293 If your kids have ever stuck out their tongues at a dish you've prepared, here's your chance to turn the tables — by serving up a couple of silly cold-cut sandwiches.

INGREDIENTS

Mayonnaise and mustard

Sandwich roll

Cold cuts, sliced raw vegetables, and softened cream cheese

Spread mayonnaise and mustard on the bottom half of a sandwich roll. Add a slice of ham or another cold cut. Then fold a second slice of meat so that it resembles a tongue and lay it across the bun, as shown.

Now create a face on the bun top using sliced raw vegetables, olives, and cherry tomatoes for features and cream cheese for glue. (The cheese sticks best if you first blot dry the veggies.)

Finally, use a potato peeler or grater to create long carrot curls to pile on top of the sandwich, or push bell pepper slices into the bun for a spiky hairdo.

Pinwheel Burritos

294 Even preschoolers can assemble these high-protein, no-cook burritos. Lay a tortilla on a clean countertop. Using a table knife, spread 2 heaping tablespoons of refried beans evenly over the tortilla. Then add 1 heaping tablespoon of salsa, if desired, and sprinkle with 1 heaping tablespoon of grated Monterey Jack cheese. Roll up the tortilla tightly. Place the roll seam side down and slice it with a sharp knife (parents only) into four pinwheels. Tightly wrap the burrito in foil or plastic, twist the ends, and pack in a lunch box. Eat cold.

Pack Your Own Lunch

To make packing lunches fun for her two sons, FamilyFun *reader Dee Martin of Cleveland established a system. She bought three plastic baskets and filled one with fruits, another with vegetables, and a third with snacks and desserts. Dee lets the boys choose one item from each basket for their lunch bags, then she adds a sandwich. The kids like to be in charge, and the system is earning rave reviews.*

Hard-boiled Egg Mice

295 With chive tails, radish ears, and olive eyes, a hard-boiled egg gets transformed into a whimsical pair of mice (that like to be served a wedge of Swiss cheese, please).

INGREDIENTS

1   **egg**

1   **black olive**

1   **radish**

2   **fresh chives**

1   **tiny Swiss cheese wedge**

Slice the egg in half lengthwise and place the halves yolk side down on a plate. Slice tiny black olive eyes and radish ears. Then make small slits in the egg halves for the eyes and ears and push in the olives and radishes. Add chive tails and a wedge of cheese. Makes 2 mice.

Lunch Box Fun & Games

296 How about a round of lunchtime tic-tac-toe? We got this idea from Jo Ella Graney of Fort Wayne, Indiana, whose kids love it. Stick dry-erase paper (we used Con-Tact Memo-board) on the inside lid of your child's lunch box to instantly transform it into an erasable board. It can be wiped clean with a napkin or paper towel.

Kitchen Projects

179

Edible Art

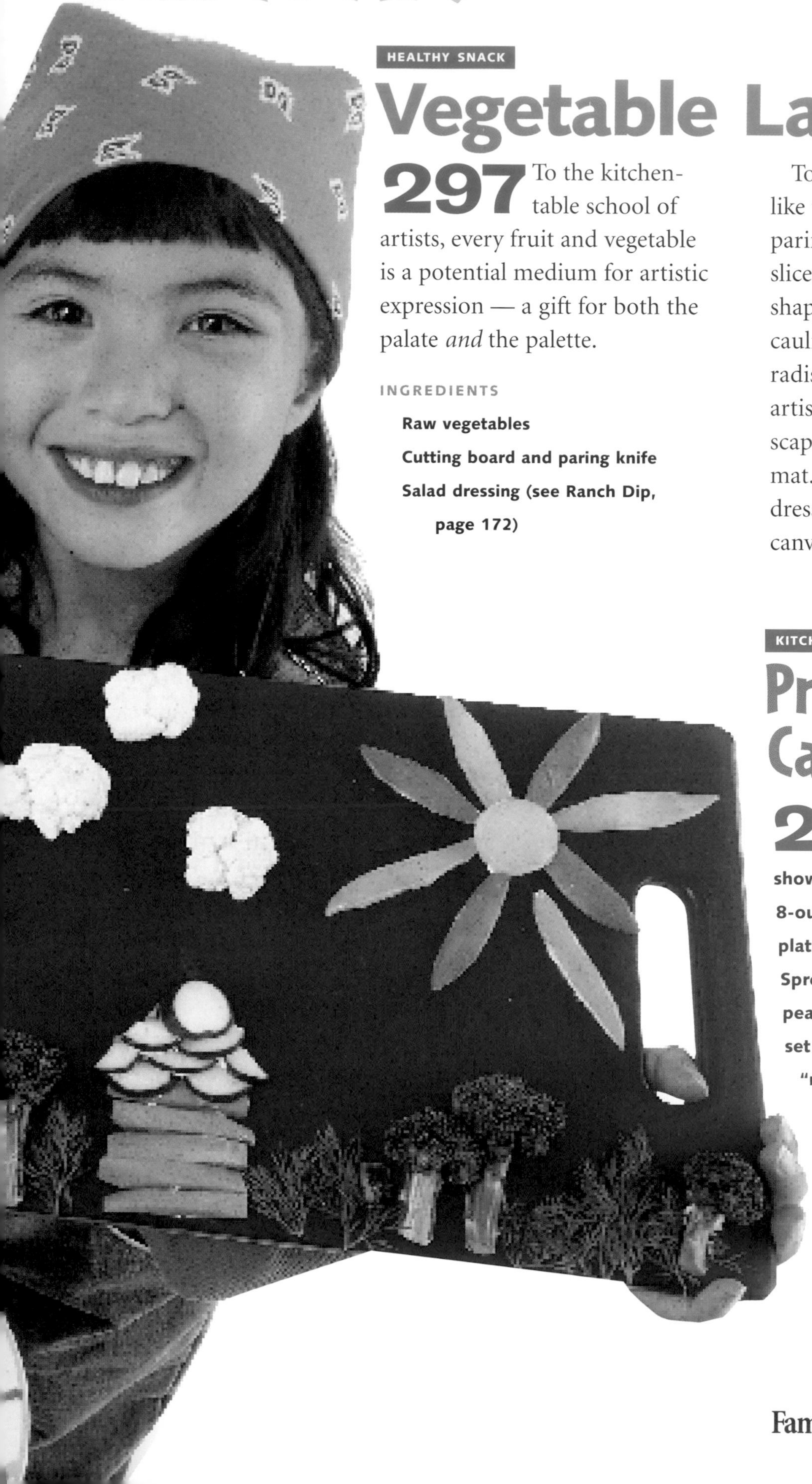

HEALTHY SNACK

Vegetable Landscape

297 To the kitchen-table school of artists, every fruit and vegetable is a potential medium for artistic expression — a gift for both the palate *and* the palette.

INGREDIENTS

- **Raw vegetables**
- **Cutting board and paring knife**
- **Salad dressing (see Ranch Dip, page 172)**

To make a vegetable landscape like the one shown here, use a paring knife (parents only) to slice raw vegetables into various shapes (bell pepper sunrays, cauliflower clouds, broccoli trees, radish-slice shingles). Your young artist can then design her landscape on a cutting board or place mat. Provide a bowl of salad dressing for dip, and this colorful canvas becomes a nutritious snack.

KITCHEN CRAFT

Pretzel Log Cabin

298 **To make a log cabin snack like the one shown on page 168, staple shut an 8-ounce milk carton and affix it to a plate with a dab of peanut butter. Spread a moderately thick layer of peanut butter all over the carton and set thin pretzel sticks into the "mortar." Fashion doors and windows from shorter sticks. Finally, shingle the roof with pretzel nuggets.**

Dough Sculpture

299 For sheer sensory pleasure, few art materials can rival fresh bread dough. We used the following recipe to bake a turtle bread with a crisscross shell and raisin eyes. Artists should, of course, feel free to sculpt anything.

INGREDIENTS

2	teaspoons active dry yeast
1	cup warm water
2	teaspoons sugar or honey
$3/4$	teaspoon salt
2	teaspoons vegetable oil
$2^{1}/_2$	to 3 cups all-purpose flour

Dissolve the yeast in warm water. Whisk in the sugar or honey, salt, and oil. Slowly stir in the flour and, as it becomes harder to stir, turn the dough onto a lightly floured countertop. Dust the dough with flour and knead it by folding it in half and pressing it with the palm of your hand. Continue to knead until the dough springs back when you lightly poke it with your finger. Form it into a ball, place it in a lightly greased bowl, and cover it with a clean towel or plastic wrap. Let it rise in a warm place for 30 minutes (it's risen enough if it doesn't spring back when you poke it with your finger).

Punch down the dough and sculpt it as you like. (For our turtle, we joined six balls, etched the shell with a knife, and stuck on raisin eyes.) Cover your finished sculpture with plastic wrap and allow the dough to rise again for 30 minutes.

Heat the oven to 375°. Lightly brush the dough sculpture with egg wash (an egg whisked with 1 tablespoon of water) and bake for 25 minutes or until golden brown.

Cookie Painting

300 Sugar cookie dough makes the perfect canvas for edible art. Cream together 1 cup of softened butter and $3/4$ cup of sugar until fluffy, then beat in 1 large egg and $3/4$ teaspoon of vanilla extract. Stir in $2^3/4$ cups of flour that has been sifted with $3/4$ teaspoon of baking soda. Form the dough into two balls (add 1 tablespoon of water if it's too crumbly), cover each with plastic wrap, and flatten. Refrigerate for 1 hour, then roll out to a $1/4$-inch thickness and cut it into six 4- by 6-inch canvases. Place them on a greased baking sheet.

Blend an egg yolk with five or six drops of food coloring; paint the cookies with this mixture. Bake in a preheated 350° oven for 8 to 10 minutes or until golden brown.

Dinner's Ready

Color Your Pasta

301 Give noodles a brilliant new hue. Mix 3 to 4 tablespoons of rubbing alcohol with a dab of food coloring paste (a parent's job), then pour the mixture over uncooked pasta, gently mixing it all together. Let the pasta dry on a cookie sheet, then it's ready to thread onto pipe cleaners, as we did with this spacey-looking alien.

PASTA DINNER

Bake a Spaghetti Pie

302 This crowd-pleaser, which begins with leftover spaghetti and store-bought tomato sauce, is easy enough for a child to make for dinner.

INGREDIENTS

- **4** cups leftover spaghetti
- **1 1/2** cups tomato sauce
- **1/2** cup grated Parmesan cheese
- Fresh basil, snipped with scissors
- **1/2** cup grated mozzarella cheese

Heat the oven to 350°. Grease a 9-inch pie pan with olive oil. Place the spaghetti and the sauce in a large bowl and stir until the noodles are coated. Stir in the Parmesan cheese and basil. Spread the spaghetti around the pie pan and pat it down with the back of a wooden spoon. Sprinkle the mozzarella cheese on top. Bake for 20 to 30 minutes or until brown and crispy on top. Cut into wedges and serve with extra Parmesan and sauce. Serves 4.

My Favorite Recipes

"My husband and I love to cook, so naturally we've encouraged our son, Scott, to help in the kitchen. Now that he's five, he definitely has preferences for certain recipes. I've started writing them down in a notebook, with anecdotes about when we made them or what Scott said. (For instance, I included his quote, 'I like crummy snacks better, Mom,' meaning, of course, those snacks, like brownies, that make crumbs.) When Scott grows up, he'll have a one-of-a-kind cookbook filled with recipes and memories."

— Chandra Peters, Honolulu, Hawaii

Homemade Butter

303 Fill a clean plastic jar halfway with whipping cream. Drop in two or three clean marbles and screw the lid on tightly. Shake the jar for 10 to 15 minutes. First the liquid will turn to whipped cream, then it will separate into a thin fluid and a yellow blob of butter. Wrap the butter in a clean dish towel, squeeze out the remaining liquid, and enjoy.

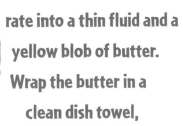

Make Your Own Hero

304 Be a hero at your neighborhood picnic or potluck with this fun idea.

INGREDIENTS

Long loaf of bread

Deli meats and cheese

Lettuce, tomatoes, and condiments

Start with the longest sandwich loaf you can find (or special-order one from a bakery).

Have each guest pick up one or two ingredients on the way to the party. Provide plenty of tasty condiments, and hoagie making is sure to be the hit of the day.

Snowman Sloppy Joes

305 Your kids will get a big kick out of these entertaining — and yummy — dinner guests. The sloppy joe has been a favorite for decades, and it's still supremely comforting fare.

INGREDIENTS

1	tablespoon vegetable oil
1	medium onion, diced
1	medium green bell pepper, diced
1	pound ground beef
1	8-ounce can tomato sauce
1/3	cup ketchup
2	teaspoons Worcestershire sauce
1/2	teaspoon chili powder
1/4	teaspoon each salt and pepper
12	biscuits or hamburger buns
	Decorations, such as mushrooms, zucchini, carrots, olives, scallion rings, and grated cheese

In a large frying pan, heat the oil over medium heat. Add the onion and diced pepper and sauté for 5 minutes or until soft. Add the ground beef, breaking it into pieces with a spatula. Sauté it until brown. Drain the fat.

Add the tomato sauce, ketchup, Worcestershire sauce, chili powder, salt, and pepper and stir well.

Cook over low heat for 3 to 5 minutes.

Meanwhile, heat the biscuits, if desired, and slice each one in half. For each snowman, arrange the bottom halves of three biscuits on a plate. Spoon the sloppy joe mixture on top of each half. Top each joe with another biscuit half.

Set out ingredients for decorating the snowmen and let the kids get creative making clothing, facial features, and so on.

Makes 4 snowmen.

Set Out a Place Mat Template

306 Take a few minutes to make our table-setting place mat, and your child will be ready to help at mealtime. Fashioned from shapes of colored paper that show the proper locations for the

plate and silverware, this mat effortlessly teaches the fine art of setting the table. Kids will feel good about being able to help out, and they'll get practice in following a diagram. We made our place mat from colored drawing paper tacked together with glue, then laminated on both sides with Con-Tact paper.

Pizza With Pizzazz

307 When it comes to food that is universally adored by kids, nothing rivals pizza. And with store-bought dough and sauce, it's a snap to make your own.

INGREDIENTS

- 1¹/₂ **pounds store-bought pizza dough**
- 1 **cup homemade or store-bought tomato sauce**
- 2¹/₂ **cups grated mozzarella cheese**
- 2¹/₂ **cups grated Muenster cheese**
  Assorted toppings (sautéed mushrooms or onions, diced or thinly sliced bell peppers, pitted and sliced black olives, blanched broccoli florets, pepperoni)

Heat the oven to 450°.

Divide the pizza dough in two. On a lightly floured work surface, use a rolling pin to roll each portion into a 12-inch round. Place the crusts on two lightly oiled baking sheets.

Spread a thin layer of sauce on each crust — not too much, or your pizza will become soggy.

Top your pizzas with the mozzarella and Muenster cheeses and garnish with the toppings of your choice. Bake 12 to 15 minutes, or until the crusts are golden underneath. Makes two 12-inch pizzas.

Pizza of the Sea

To make the friendly fish pictured below, we divided the pizza dough into thirds and shaped each third into a fish. We then covered each fish with sauce and cheese and overlapped pepperoni slices (about 20 per fish) to make scales. We added an olive eye to each, then baked the fish as directed at left. Makes 3 pizza fish.

Silly Sweets

Decorate a Cupcake

308 Here's one of our favorite secret weapons for turning around a gray day: making fancy cupcakes for no reason at all. Ahead of time, buy some cake decorating supplies: candy hearts, sparkles, decorative roses, tubes of frosting. The fancier the better. When bad moods strike, break out the supplies, along with a batch of cupcakes (store-bought for ease, if you prefer). Let your kids decorate with abandon, then celebrate the birthday of a stuffed animal or some other worthy occasion.

INGREDIENTS

Cupcakes

Assorted tubs and tubes of frosting

Assorted candy, sprinkles, and other
  edible decorations

The cupcake decorating possibilities are limited only by your child's imagination. Some of our favorites include:

Pajama Party Kids. Frost a cupcake white. Use a toothpick dipped in melted chocolate to add a face and hair to a Mentos fruit candy. Snip fruit stripe gum with scissors to make pajamas.

Fish Food. Frost a cupcake blue and white. Cut fruit leather into a fish, add an eye and mouth, and stick on blue M&M's Minis for bubbles.

To-dye-for Cupcakes. Frost a cupcake with white icing and squirt on a series of concentric circles of colorful gel icings. To create the tie-dye effect, draw a toothpick through the gel, moving from the center outward, like a spiderweb.

Shamburger

309
This sneaky sandwich is a perfect prank for April Fool's Day, but tasty any time of year.

To make the cookie buns, use an electric mixer to cream 1 cup of margarine with 1 cup of sugar until fluffy. Add 2 eggs and beat well. Stir in 1 teaspoon of vanilla extract. Sift together 2½ cups of flour, ½ teaspoon of salt, and 1½ teaspoons of baking powder, then beat this into the creamed mixture. Drop the dough by the rounded tablespoonful onto a lightly greased baking sheet and flatten each bun slightly with the floured bottom of a glass. Brush with beaten egg, sprinkle with sesame seeds, and bake in a preheated 375° oven for 10 minutes or until golden. Cool the cookies on a wire rack.

To assemble the burgers, choose two cookies that are about the same size. Spread one with ketchup or mustard (red or yellow icing), add a burger-size peppermint patty, and sprinkle with lettuce (shake 1 cup of shredded coconut in a plastic bag with a few drops of green food coloring). Add another squirt of your favorite icing condiment before placing the second bun on top. Makes approximately 12 burgers.

Cinderella Cake

310
Serve this fairy-tale cake at a birthday celebration or school party, and your child and her guests are sure to have a ball.

WHAT YOU NEED

2 boxes of cake mix

Pink and white frosting and tubes of colored gel frosting

Cake doll (available for about $3 at many party stores or wherever cake decorating supplies are sold)

First, prepare the cake mix according to the package directions. Bake half of the batter in a greased and floured 2½-quart Pyrex bowl and the rest in two 9-inch round cake pans according to the package directions (the bowl cake may take about an hour).

Once they've cooled, stack the two round cakes and then the bowl cake (flat side down) on a serving plate to form a skirt, and frost them white. When the frosting firms up (you may have to chill the cake for a while), frost the upper two thirds of the skirt pink. Pipe on decorative gel trim. Then press the waist of the cake doll into the center of the cake. Dress her in a frosting bodice, and she's ready to make her debut.

Cookie Puppets

311 Atop a lollipop stick and decorated with candies, the classic sugar cookie quickly becomes a great entertainer. Roll out your favorite sugar cookie dough (see ours, page 181) and use a wide-mouthed glass to cut out faces. Place each round on an ungreased baking sheet and insert a lollipop stick in the center of each cookie; chill for 30 minutes. Bake the cookies in a preheated 350° oven for 8 to 10 minutes or until golden brown around the edges. Cool on the baking sheets for 5 minutes and then remove to wire racks. Set out tubes of decorators' frosting and assorted candies and let your kids add facial features before staging a delicious show.

Ice-cream Castle

312 Give your little princes and princesses their just desserts — a majestic ice-cream castle.

WHAT YOU NEED

- 1 quart of vanilla or coffee ice cream
- A plastic sand castle mold, 5 inches tall and 5¼ inches wide
- 1 cup of sugar mixed with 2 teaspoons of cinnamon
- Candy seashells and pebbles, gummy octopuses, and a paper flag

Let the ice cream soften slightly at room temperature, then pack it firmly into your mold. Cover the top with plastic wrap and freeze it overnight.

Unmold the castle by quickly dipping it into a pot of hot water. Top it with a foil-covered jelly roll pan, invert it onto the counter, and lift off the mold.

Working quickly, sprinkle the cinnamon sugar "sand" on the sides and top of the castle. Freeze until frozen solid (at least 3 hours).

Just before serving, roll the sides of the castle in the remaining cinnamon sugar (work over foil). Set the castle on a serving plate, sprinkle the top with more of the cinnamon sugar, and spread what's left on the plate for a beach. Add the candy seashells and pebbles and the gummy octopuses. Finally, top the castle with the paper flag. Makes eight ½-cup servings.

Make Brownie Sundaes

313 Want to surprise your kids with a festive snack-tivity on a long, gray afternoon? Set up a sundae bar, complete with brownies, ice cream, hot fudge sauce, whipped cream, nuts, sprinkles, candy toppings, and cherries. Arrange the ingredients and sundae glasses or bowls on a table low enough for kids to see and reach, then invite the kids to build their own brownie sundaes (an adult can scoop the ice cream).

Zany Jell-O

315 Here's how to add some wiggle room to your house.
Lollipops: Mix two 3-ounce packages of gelatin with 1¼ cups of boiling water (parents only). Pour into four 5-ounce paper cups and refrigerate for 3 hours. Peel off the cups, cut each pop horizontally into three slices, and push a straw into each.
Pinwheels: Mix one 3-ounce package of gelatin with ½ cup of warm water in a microwave-safe bowl. Microwave for 1½ minutes, stir to dissolve, then add 1½ cups of mini marshmallows and microwave for 1 minute or until almost melted. Stir until smooth. Pour into an 8- or 9-inch square pan coated with cooking spray. Refrigerate for 45 minutes or until set. Starting at one edge, roll up the gelatin tightly. With the seam side down, cut into ½-inch slices.

Brownie Pizza

314 Topped with red frosting "sauce" and white chocolate "cheese," this sweet look-alike is fun to make and sure to please.

INGREDIENTS

1	box brownie mix
2½	cups confectioners' sugar
½	cup butter (1 stick), softened
2½	tablespoons milk
1	teaspoon vanilla extract
	Red food coloring paste (available at kitchen and party supply stores)
6	ounces white chocolate
	Assorted candies

Prepare the brownie mix according to the package directions, but bake it in a lightly greased 12-inch pizza pan for 20 to 30 minutes. Let it cool.

For the sauce, cream the confectioners' sugar and butter in a large bowl. Add the milk and vanilla extract and beat until smooth. Add red food coloring until you have the desired shade (think tomato sauce). Use a spatula or knife to spread the sauce evenly over the pizza.

Add the toppings. For cheese, roughly chop or grate (adults only) the white chocolate. Sprinkle it over the frosting and add other toppings — M&M's, chocolate chips, butterscotch chips, or any favorite candies.

Slice with a pizza wheel and serve. Serves 16.

Strawberry Shortcake Snake

316 Your kids will get a kick out of helping to shape these *berry* reptilian shortcakes.

INGREDIENTS

- 2 **cups all-purpose flour**
- 2 **tablespoons confectioners' sugar**
- 4 **teaspoons baking powder**
- ³/₄ **teaspoon salt**
- ¹/₂ **cup margarine (1 stick)**
- 1 **cup milk**
- 1 **quart strawberries**
- 2 **cups sweetened whipped cream**
  M&M's Minis
  Green fruit leather

Heat the oven to 400°. Sift the flour, sugar, baking powder, and salt into a bowl. Cut in the margarine with a pastry cutter until the mixture crumbles, then stir in the milk. Turn the dough onto a floured surface and pat it into a 1-inch-thick rectangle. Slice it into four 1½- by 8-inch strips, place them on an ungreased baking sheet, and mold into S shapes. Bake for 10 to 12 minutes, until the bottoms are golden brown. Cool on a rack.

Slice the shortcakes in half lengthwise. Set aside four whole strawberries. Slice the rest and arrange some on the bottom half of each shortcake, then cover with its top. Spread on whipped cream and sliced strawberry scales. Give each snake a whole strawberry head, M&M's Minis eyes, and a fruit leather tongue. Serves 4.

Melt-in-your-mouth Melon

317 Just right to slice and serve at a poolside gathering or summer dinner party, this easy-to-make mock watermelon combines three great flavors: fresh honeydew melon, tangy raspberry sherbert, and chocolate. First, refrigerate a ripe honeydew melon for an hour or two or until it is well

chilled. Cut the cold melon in half, scoop out the seeds, and pack the center of each half with sherbert. Slice each of the filled halves into four wedges. Press chocolate chip "watermelon seeds" into the sherbert on each slice and serve immediately. Makes 8 servings.

Pig Out on Apples

318 Disguised as peewee porkers, these are apples kids will go hog-wild over.

Turn an apple on its side. Insert one end of a toothpick into a gumdrop and stick the other end into the bottom of the apple to form a snout. Use two toothpicks broken in half to affix four gumdrops as feet. Set clove nostrils in the snout and clove eyes above it.

Next, twist off the stem, poke a hole with a toothpick, and insert an inch-long piece of shoestring licorice to make a tail. Finally, cut a piece of fruit leather into a 1- by ½-inch rectangle, then cut it again on the diagonal to form two equal-size triangles. Affix the triangles with small pieces of toothpick to create ears, then bend over the upper portion of each triangle to cover the spot where the toothpick shows.

Note: Before your kids pig out on these apple snacks, remind them to remove the toothpicks and cloves.

Spaghetti and Malt Balls

319 If you want to outdo your child's best pranks, you've got to use your noodles. Just serve our foolproof Italian feast, and the payoff couldn't be sweeter.

Cook up some spaghetti. Place a shortcake biscuit, half of a cupcake, or a half slice of pound cake on a plate.

Prepare about 3 cups of your favorite buttercream frosting, spoon it into a decorating tube fitted with a large circular tip, and pipe it in a looping fashion around the sides of the biscuit or cake — do not frost the top.

Top it with secret sauce. Spoon strawberry ice-cream sauce on top of the biscuit or cake to cover. Drizzle some over the spaghetti as well.

Make mini meatballs. Use a butter knife to rough up the surface of two or three chocolate-covered malt balls. Place them atop the sauce.

Sprinkle with grated cheese. Crush a handful of blanched almonds or walnuts in a blender, then sprinkle the pieces over the sauce and meatballs.

Toast some garlic bread. First, toast some coconut (for the garlic) in a shallow baking pan at 350°, stirring often, for 8 to 10 minutes or until golden. For butter, melt ¼ cup of white chocolate chips in a double boiler — or heat them in a microwave for about 1½ minutes at half power and then stir them until smooth. Spread the melted white chocolate on toasted lady fingers. Top with the toasted coconut and, for parsley, green sprinkles.

Celebrate an International Holiday, page 213

CHAPTER EIGHT

Brain Boosters

Inspiring activities that bring out

your child's natural curiosity

WHEN IT COMES to cheering up a rainy afternoon, multiplication tables are unlikely, we know, to be first on your child's list of activities. Baking cookies, on the other hand, just might be. What do the two have in common? Math skills, of course! But while straight-up arithmetic smacks of homework, cookie baking sneaks in skills deliciously. It's what we call stealth learning — a fun, casual way to encourage kids' curiosity about the world around them.

While helping to measure ingredients for a favorite recipe, your child starts to get the scoop on fractions. As she watches the backyard bird feeder, she peers into the secret lives of robins and wrens and discovers the thrill of scientific observation. These everyday learning moments often seem to come about by chance, but there are ways to make sure they happen more regularly.

What works best? Keep learning playful. You've probably noticed that some of the most memorable learning experiences take place when you and your children are just enjoying each other's company. The biggest hits don't have the feel of homework (for child or parent) but are simply new ways to have a good time together. Here are some of our favorite ideas — inspiration, we hope, to make learning fun in your home.

Encourage your kids' passions. Whenever you can, blur the boundaries between learning and pleasure. Does your child love writing stories? Help your budding author decorate a special journal and create a nest of pillows for him to write in. Got a kid who's wild for dinosaurs? Take a road trip to the nearest natural history museum or visit the library for some books on Jurassic life.

Show your own love of learning. Modeling enthusiastic learning habits is probably the best way to inspire a child. Get out the dictionary when your novel presents you with a word you don't know. Pore over the atlas to

Get Global Perspective, page 212

Learning Activity Bingo

Want to keep your kids energized about learning? Try this activity-based version of bingo. Just set up a game board that includes all of your child's school subjects and write an activity in each square. The squares in the science category, for example, might ask your child to do a fun experiment, identify a new wildflower, or find an unfamiliar constellation. Mark every completed activity with a sticker and determine a prize for each bingo. Why not keep stealth learning in mind when you reward your winning contestant? Try a trip to a discovery museum.

Invent units of measure, page 204

further your understanding of international news. Bring along a field guide when you set out for a hike. Stay curious, and your child will inevitably follow suit.

Get involved at school. Volunteer in the library once a week, teach the class a family recipe, or tag along on field trips — the students will benefit from your skills and interests. In addition, a regular visit to the classroom will give you important information about what, and how, your child is learning.

Make your home a classroom. Think about organizing your house so that a variety of learning materials are readily accessible to your kids. Besides stocking your child's bookshelves with fiction and nonfiction, keep a telescope and an astronomy guide by the window, a box of utensils and containers earmarked for science experiments in the pantry, an up-to-date globe in the family room, and a good encyclopedia CD-ROM near the computer.

Science Experiments

KITCHEN EXPERIMENT

Penciled In

320 Poke a hole in a plastic bag filled with water, and you're sure to spring a leak, right? Not necessarily. Try this!

MATERIALS

- **Plastic bag**
- **Water**
- **Sharpened pencils**

Fill the bag three quarters of the way with water and then knot the top. With one hand, hold the bag over a sink. In one swift motion, push a pencil, point first, straight through one side of the bag and out the other. No water should leak out. See how many more pencils you can poke through without causing a leak.

The explanation behind this mysterious feat involves the elasticity of the plastic. When you pierce the bag, the plastic stretches and then breaks open just enough for the pencil to fit through. The glovelike fit leaves no room for the water to pass through.

THE SENSES

Trick Your Buds

321 Without taste buds on our tongues (and a sense of smell), we couldn't tell jelly beans from lima beans. Most scientists think the tongue "specializes" in four tastes: sweet, salty, sour, and bitter. Slice some citrus fruit and touch different parts of your tongue with it. Is the taste most distinct on the sour sections? Now rinse your mouth and try again with a bit of banana. Does it taste best on the sweet section?

Bitter
Salty
Sweet
Sour

SCIENCE TRICK

Raisin Races

322 This wacky game demonstrates some fascinating science — and refreshes your kids with a cold drink. Carefully fill glasses with equal amounts of a clear carbonated beverage, trying to minimize the fizzing. On cue, everyone drops in a raisin, which should sink to

the bottom, then — as the carbon dioxide bubbles gather on the raisin's surface, increasing its buoyancy — quickly rise to the surface. First raisin to the top wins.

195

A Glass of Air

323 This trick offers graphic proof of how much air and water don't like each other: they won't even share the same glass.

First, wedge a paper napkin tightly in the bottom of a clear plastic glass or cup. Now turn the glass so its rim is down and sink it straight into the water, being careful not to tilt the rim. If the trick is done right, the trapped air will prevent the water from entering the glass, and the napkin will stay high and dry. **Note:** The diving bells of old operated on the same principle. In essence, they were huge metal cups that held a bubble of air for the divers to breathe.

Amazing Eggs-periment

324 You'd think that forcing a hard-boiled egg through the neck of a bottle would be near impossible. But here's how you can use physics to make it happen.

MATERIALS

- Peeled hard-boiled egg
- Glass returnable milk bottle (ask at natural food stores)
- Bowl of cold water
- Hot tap water
- Dish gloves

First, try it yourself: set the egg on the mouth of the bottle and try to push it inside without smooshing the egg. Give up? Now place the egg in a bowl of cold water. Meanwhile, place the milk bottle under hot tap water for a minute or so, letting it fill. Then, wearing dish gloves to protect your hands, empty the water down the drain (a parent's job). Quickly place the egg, tapered end down, on the mouth of the bottle and watch carefully. The egg slowly gets sucked into the bottle with a satisfying *thunk*. That's because the hot air inside the bottle is less dense (and thus at a lower pressure) than the cooler outside air. The difference creates a suction that pulls the squishy egg through the bottle neck.

Lava Lite

325 This seventies-style retro-vention uses the principles of immiscible liquids (fluids that just won't mix) and density to create the Lava Lite, a homemade version of that classic mind-expanding device, the Lava lamp.

MATERIALS

Glass jar

Water with food coloring added

¹/₃ cup vegetable oil

Shaker filled with salt

Fill the jar with 3 inches of the colored water. Add the oil and let the layers settle. Shake in salt while you count to five. The oil and salt should form a glob and sink to the bottom of the jar, but after a short while, the oil should float back to the top. Add salt again to watch the action repeat.

Here's what's going on: At first, the oil floats on top because it's less dense than water. The salt, however, is denser than the water. When you

shake it onto the oil, it drags a glob to the jar bottom. There, the salt dissolves in the water and can no longer hold down the oil blob, which rises back to the surface.

Rubber Blubber

326 Invite your young scientists to see what happens when glue molecules interact with a borax solution – you end up with a rubbery substance that actually bounces!

Directions: Combine 1 quart of water and 1 tablespoon of borax in a large jar. Stir well and let the mix stand for a few minutes. Next, fill a disposable cup three quarters of the way with the borax solution. Stir in a few drops of food coloring. Add white glue (in a thin, steady stream), stirring continuously. Keep adding glue until a large stringy mass wraps around the spoon. Pull the mass off the spoon and drop it into a container of cold water. Then remove the Rubber Blubber and, with dry hands, squeeze it for a minute or so to get rid of the air bubbles. Now roll it into a ball and see how high it will bounce. Store the Rubber Blubber in a plastic bag.

Rocket Balloons

327 This activity, which turns balloons into rockets, is great for teaching kids about Isaac Newton's Third Law of Motion (for every action, there is an equal and opposite reaction). That's because the balloon gets its lifting thrust from air rushing out of the neck. For each rocket, securely tape one end of a long string to the ceiling. Thread a drinking straw onto the string, then stretch the string taut to the floor and tie it to a weight or tape it down. Have each kid inflate a long, torpedo-shaped balloon and keep the neck pinched shut while you tape it to the straw. While the kids hold their balloons near the floor, count down to takeoff and see whose rocket goes fastest and highest.

Volcano in a Bottle

328 More than 2,000 square miles of Hawaii's Big Island have been covered with the lava flows of Mauna Loa, the world's biggest volcano. Here's a vivid way to show your child how and why a volcano erupts.

MATERIALS

- Small plastic water bottle
- Warm water
- Red food coloring
- ¼ cup vinegar
- Heaping teaspoon baking soda

Set the bottle in your sink and fill it three quarters of the way with warm water. Add a few drops of red food coloring and the vinegar. Now, using a kitchen funnel held just above the bottle top, quickly add the baking soda. The mixture will instantly fizz and overflow from the bottle.

Inform your child that vinegar and baking soda together produce carbon dioxide — the very gas that makes hot liquid rock beneath the earth's surface erupt from Mauna Loa and other volcanoes.

Magnetic Attractions

329 Here are a couple of simple experiments that will let your kids explore the world of magnet magic.

Compass in a Bowl: Magnetize a needle by repeatedly stroking it in one direction with the end of a magnet. Cut a slice of cork, set it in a bowl of water, and place the needle on top. The needle will slowly turn to align itself with the lines of force of the earth's magnetic field.

Flying Fish: Cut a fish shape from lightweight paper and affix a paper clip. Tie a length of thread to the clip. Tape the opposite end of the thread to the inner bottom of a glass jar (one that has a metal lid), adjusting the thread length so that the clip almost (but not quite) reaches the rim. Screw on the lid and place a magnet on top of it. Then invert the jar so that the clip is caught in the magnetic field. Finally, turn the jar upright again, and your fish will be flying.

Eyewitnessed

330 Pictures, written words, and other things we see account for two thirds of the information we store in our brains. But sometimes what we think we see isn't real. Here are a few ways our eyes play tricks on us.

Seeing Spots: Color a nickel-size red dot on white paper. Place this sheet atop another blank sheet, then set them under a bright light and stare at the dot for 30 seconds. Remove the top sheet and stare at the blank paper. A green spot will appear. Staring at the dot fatigues the cone cells on your retina that see red. Look away, and the ones that see green (a complementary color to red) briefly overcompensate, so you see a "ghost" image.

Missing Money: Place a quarter on a table and set an empty glass jar on top of it. Looking through the side of the jar, focus on the coin while you pour in enough water to nearly fill the jar. The coin will seemingly disappear. Here's why: the empty jar lets light bounce straight from the coin to your eyes. When the jar is filled, the water refracts light, bending it away from your eyes and making the coin invisible.

Now You See It: Form a circle with your thumb and index finger and hold it at arm's length. Looking through the circle, focus on an object. Without moving, close one eye and then the other. One eye will see the object through the circle; the other won't. That's because one eye is dominant and does the job of focusing your gaze.

Stir Up an Incredible Edible Lens

331 Next time you're making a light-colored batch of gelatin dessert, fill the bottom of a wineglass with about an inch of the liquid. Refrigerate the gelatin for at least 4 hours. When it is completely set, run hot water over the outside of the glass and use a warm, wet knife to gently loosen the gelatin. Now invert the gelatin, flat side down, onto a piece of damp, clear plastic wrap — and look before you eat! Try moving your jiggly lens different distances from a newspaper or other objects you want to magnify.

Reading

Page Savers

332 Reading can be lots of fun — until you lose your page! These clip-on place keepers come in handy.

Bead Bangles: Tie thin cording to a paper clip. String on beads or charms. Then double-knot the loose end to keep the beads from slipping off.

Fuzzy Braid: Bend three different-colored pipe cleaners in half and hook them over one end of a paper clip. Pair up and braid the like-colored ends and pinch together the bottoms.

Start a Book Club

333 A kids' book club can relieve boredom on two fronts. First, it offers a fun weekly (or monthly) occasion to look forward to, and second, it is a great incentive to read stories that jump-start the imagination.

To make lighter work, partner up with a friend, then send out invitations that include the title of the first book (ask your librarian for a recommendation) and a weekly time to meet. Before each club meeting, have all the kids read the same book (or specified chapters).

Then, when members get together, they can share their thoughts — and some snacks too.

To get things started, the host child might want to make a list of five or so discussion questions (What was your favorite part? Who was the best character?). Or, if the readers are younger, you can read aloud while they listen or draw along to the story. If the kids like, you might consider choosing a loose theme for the books — for example, all wintertime stories or books from everyone's favorite series of the moment.

Play Dictionary

334 Words rule in this bluffing game. One person reads a word from the dictionary that he thinks no one knows. While he writes down the real definition, the other players write fakes that sound wacky enough to be true. Next, he reads out all of the definitions. Whoever picks the real one gets 1 point. If no one does, the chooser gets 2 points. Now it's someone else's turn to pick a word.

Late-night Reading

Bookworms and night owls unite in this special literary treat. Give your kids a flashlight and let them stay awake later than usual to read in the dark. They'll start looking forward to bedtime, plus they'll get in some extra reading time. Try ten minutes on weeknights and a longer (or unlimited) time on weekends.

Home Library

"My daughter, Cailin, wanted to start her own library, so I scoured yard sales and used-book sales and found about 50 books (the average price per book was 25 cents). Then I bought a date stamp and ink pad, and with the help of our school librarian, I got book pockets and book cards. Cailin, her sister, Erin, and their friends have spent hours checking out books and hosting story-time at our new neighborhood library."

— Connie Lowry
Gastonia, North Carolina

Bring Books to Life

335 A great book doesn't have to end when you've read the last page. As the following examples show, the simplest activity is often all it takes to keep the story alive in a child's imagination.

Cook a storybook recipe: Make chocolate sauce after reading *Charlie and the Chocolate Factory*, bake old-fashioned breads or cookies from *The Little House on the Prairie*, or serve a tiny buffet — an apple, a tea sandwich, an oatmeal cookie — à la *The Very Hungry Caterpillar*.

Put on a teddy bear picnic: Read *Winnie-the-Pooh, Paddington Bear,* or *Corduroy* books and have everyone bring their bears to a picnic in the park.

Grow a garden: Be inspired by *The Lorax* and plant a tree to take care of the earth and beautify your yard. Or follow Mary Lenox's lead in *The Secret Garden* and bring new life to an old flowerbed.

Go on a treasure hunt: Design a map according to the storybook: a deserted island from *Treasure Island* or Neverland from *Peter Pan*.

Make a craft: Fashion a small raft out of sticks after reading *The Adventures of Tom Sawyer* or make Harry Potteresque wizard hats with poster board and sticker stars.

Writing Games

ACTIVITY KIT

Writing Basket

336 This stationery supply station will come in handy whenever your kids want to write a letter or send a thank-you note.

MATERIALS

- **Stationery supplies**
- **Wire mesh or plastic desk organizer**

First, let your kids help pick out a cool assortment of postcards, notecards, stickers, stamps, pencils, and pens. Then fill out a personal calendar book together, recording important addresses, birthdays, anniversaries, and any other significant dates. Put all the write stuff in a tidy organizer and keep it in an accessible place. You might even set aside a special time each week and call it "Write a Note Night."

WORD GAME

Snip a Silly Sentence

337 Even kids who think they don't like to write will enjoy this playful word game. Give everyone a pair of scissors, blank paper, a glue stick, and a part of the newspaper. Tell them they have to construct a silly sentence using any words or phrases they see in the headlines. The punnier and funnier, the better! Don't forget to read your snippy sentences aloud and post them on the fridge or family bulletin board.

He loves his steady progress in **making** students just take the day off

Honoring a celebrated brother is The ultimate victory

Swamp Bat may help kids to get money

FAMILYFUN READER IDEA

The Alphabet Museum

"Nicolas, my kindergartner, needed an entertaining way to learn his letters and start recognizing words, so we hit upon the idea of setting up an Alphabet Museum. We gathered all the boxes we could find, then went looking through his toy chest for things whose names started with different letters. I wrote 'Aa' on the first box, and Nicolas found a toy airplane to put inside. I added the word airplane *to the top of the box. It took clever thinking to find an item for every box (such as a yak Beanie Baby for Y!). But when we finished, we held a grand opening and invited the rest of the family to guess what was in each box before Nicholas 'read' the word and showed us."*

— *Pat McGough-Wujcik*

In-house Mailbox

338 Getting her own mail can be really exciting for a child. A note from a friend, a card from Grandma, even junk mail is quickly opened and (here's why we're telling you this) eagerly read. The experience can be all the more special if the mail is delivered to a personalized indoor mailbox. On days when there's no real mail, you can surprise your child with a short letter or postcard you wrote yourself.

MATERIALS

> **Shoe box**
>
> **Decorative supplies (construction paper, glitter, paint, stamps, photographs)**
>
> **Red poster board**
>
> **Paper fastener**
>
> **Scissors**

Have your child decorate a shoe box using construction paper, glitter, paint, stamps, photographs, and other supplies of her liking. Cut a flag out of poster board and attach to the box with the paper fastener so it can be raised when someone leaves a letter. You can cut a delivery slot in the box top or merely remove the cover to deposit and retrieve mail.

Put the finished mailbox in a prominent spot and keep a pad of paper and a pencil near it. Then try to keep the mail flowing by encouraging other family members and visitors to post a friendly note whenever the mood strikes.

Words on the Fridge

339 Turn your kitchen into a learning zone. Gather your alphabet magnets, grab the dictionary, and spell out words your family doesn't ordinarily use. Now challenge everyone to incorporate them into your daily conversations.

Cooking Lessons

340 In Colonial days, when children learned the alphabet, their families celebrated by making gingerbread letters. Try it yourself by rolling out your favorite gingerbread or sugar cookie dough and cutting out a tasty batch of letters. Roll the dough flat to a $1/4$-inch thickness and let your kids cut out large letters with a butter knife (if you're lucky enough to have them, you could use alphabet cookie cutters). With a spatula, set the letters on a lightly greased baking sheet and bake them according to your recipe's directions. Once the cookies cool, your kids can spell words before they eat them. (Y-u-m would make a nice-size snack; w-o-n-d-e-r-f-u-l might be a two- or three-person job!)

Math Magic

Invent Your Own Units of Measure

341 Young kids get practice counting, and learn that numbers have meaning, when you teach them how to measure. But instead of employing a ruler or measuring tape, show them how to use their own hand or foot as a sizing-up device. Attaching your child's name to this new custom unit — calling it a Joshua foot or a Jenna hand — adds to the fun. How many Joshua feet does it take to cross the parking lot? How many Jenna hands long is the cat? With his own custom unit, your child is always equipped to "measure up"!

Par 20: Card Game

342 This game is great for improving a child's math skills. Plus, it poses an interesting challenge: scoring as few points as possible.

WHAT YOU NEED

A deck of cards (remove the jacks and kings)

Paper and a pencil

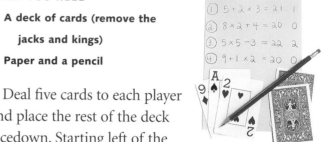

Deal five cards to each player and place the rest of the deck facedown. Starting left of the dealer, players try to make a mathematical equation totaling 20 from any three of their five cards (aces equal 1, and queens equal 0). If you have, say, 6, 3, 7, 8, and 2, one answer would be $6 \times 3 + 2 = 20$. If you succeed, you get zero points. If your equation doesn't equal exactly 20, your score for that round is the difference (higher or lower) between your total and 20. A total of 18 or 22, for example, saddles you with 2 points. After recording your equation and score, discard your used cards and draw new ones. Whoever has the lowest score after five rounds wins.

Go on a Treasure Hunt

Maribeth Knierim of Mokena, Illinois, knows few things appeal to a kid's sense of adventure more than a treasure hunt — an allure she uses to teach math to her two sons, Austin, age nine, and Max, five. The list of clues for one of her hunts might read: A. Start at the porch facing north. B. Take 4×5 steps. C. Turn left and jump $8 + 46$ times. D. Face west and skip 6×2 times. E. Look under the rock marked X. Sometimes the boys discover chocolate coins, but mostly, Maribeth says, they have a good time learning to add, multiply, and follow directions.

Tricky Triangles

343 Sometimes the key to answering a tricky math problem has everything to do with how you look at it. Take this cheesy pyramid puzzle. How many triangles can you find? One? Sixteen? More? To come up with the total number, you'll need to look at the big and little picture.

(For the answer, see page 219.)

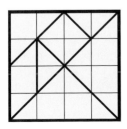

Tangram

344 The Chinese call this classic game *Qi Qiao Ban*, which translates as "seven clever pieces." To make it, repeatedly fold a square of paper in half to create 16 smaller squares, then cut the open sheet along the bold lines, as shown below, to make a square, a rhomboid, and five triangles. With the cutout shapes, you can make hundreds of designs. For starters, see if you and your kids can piece together the long-eared rabbit shown above.

Triangular Construction

345 Sometimes more is less. Take a triangle. It only has three sides, but when used in construction, it's stronger than a square. That's because a triangle spreads the force equally over its sides, which keeps it from collapsing under pressure. (That's why a pitched roof is supported by a series of wooden triangles — to keep it from caving in under heavy rain or snow.) Here's a fun — and flavorful — way your child can test the strength of triangular construction.

MATERIALS

Toothpicks

Lots of gumdrops

Push the tips of three toothpicks into three gumdrops to create a basic triangle.

With two more toothpicks and another gumdrop, attach an adjoining triangle.

Add more and more toothpick triangles to build a bridge or a tower — then test its strength by seeing how many CDs it can hold.

MONEY MATH

Mileage Money

346 In the McComas family of Reisterstown, Maryland, 12-year-old Joshua has a shot at earning some extra cash each month, but only if he does his math. He's in charge of the gas log — recording the mileage, gas price, and gallons added, and then figuring out the miles per gallon. After coming up with the monthly totals, Joshua gets to pocket any money left over in the gas budget. He's become an expert on budgeting, local gas prices, and shortcuts.

PERSPECTIVE PROJECT

Shrinking Sheep

347 You know how something huge (like a jumbo jet) looks tiny when it's far away? That phenomenon — known as perspective — is what an artist uses to create the illusion that certain drawn or painted two-dimensional objects are off in the distance. Here's a collage project that will let your child achieve the same effect.

WHAT YOU NEED

Green, blue, and white construction paper

Glue stick

Colored markers

Cut out two grassy hills from green construction paper. Glue them onto a sheet of blue paper so that the top of the first hill slightly overlaps the bottom of the second hill, and the top of the blue paper resembles the sky, as shown.

From the white paper, cut or tear out a bunch of sheep in a variety of sizes. Glue them onto the hills so that the larger ones are along the bottom edge of the landscape and the smallest are nearer the top. Then use markers to add faces and legs. Doesn't it look like your flock is wandering away?

ADDING GAME

Ball Points

348 Looking for some easy entertainment? Glue inverted jar lids on a poster board square and use markers to print numbers on them, as shown. Now take turns trying to land a rubber ball in one of the lids to earn its point value. The first person to tally 20 points or more wins.

Kids' Yard Sale

349 Want to tidy up the house and teach your kids math skills all in one fell swoop? Hold a yard sale. Ask your kids to round up all the toys, puzzles, games, and sports equipment that they are willing to part with (assuming there's not a younger sibling waiting in the wings for a coveted castoff). Give them masking tape for labeling everything with prices — ideally, no more than 25 or 50 cents an item. Hang a sign on a card table outside, set up the goods, a change box, and a pad and pencil for quick additions, and let your entrepreneurs get to work.

Start a Business

350 Do your kids want to make a little pocket money and have a lot of fun? Let them start their own business — totaling the profits might just hone their math skills. Here are some suggestions.

New leash on life: If your kid enjoys and is comfortable with handling dogs, a dog-walking business is the perfect way to spend more time with pooches.

Magnificent magnets: Snazzy magnets are useful and always in demand. Your child can add craft magnets to the backs of almost anything she dreams up — painted pebble creatures, miniature collages, mosaics, or shells.

Compu-creativity: For computer-savvy kids, print-shop-style software makes starting a mini design business easy. Sell batches of birthday greetings, a year's worth of holiday cards, stickers, or labels.

Mom-mart

Tracey Hodapp of Erie, Pennsylvania, has found an easy way to make child's play of money lessons for her two young children, Bradley, age six, and Isaac, two, and the other kids she cares for after school. Every day, the kids earn pennies, nickels, and dimes for completing work sheets and other learning activities. Then, once a week, Tracey opens her Mom-mart: a big briefcase full of stickers, pencils, candy, and other trinkets that are assigned various prices. The kids use their earnings to make purchases, so they get lots of practice understanding costs and making change.

The Natural World

HANDS-ON LEARNING

Great Gizzards

351 This activity demonstrates how birds digest their insect meals. First, explain to your child that birds swallow their food whole, then the stomach's digestive juices break it into smaller pieces. These bits then pass into a muscular organ called a gizzard, which grinds the food. Fill a sturdy plastic bag (for a gizzard) with a half cup of uncooked rolled oats. Drop in 15 marbles to simulate the small stones that birds swallow to aid digestion and seal the bag. Have your child knead the bag to mimic the contracting walls of a gizzard. Shortly, the oats will be ground into fine bits.

QUICK ACTIVITY

The Buzz on Hummingbirds

The world's smallest birds are tall on talent. The buzz that a hummingbird makes comes from the incredible speed of its beating wings — up to 80 beats a second. To help your child gauge just how fast that is, ask her to clap her hands as many times as possible for one minute. Divide that number by 60 to get the number of "beats" per second. How'd she do?

BIRD BIOLOGY

Set Up a Birding Basket

352 The sudden arrival of a colorful new visitor at a backyard bird feeder can be just the thrill that turns on a kid to the wonders of the natural world. Put together a birding basket — equipped with binoculars, guidebooks, and a birding log — and she'll be ready for bird-watching at the drop of a feather.

The National Audubon Society suggests that you furnish your basket with compact, rubber-coated binoculars; a good guidebook, such as the group's own *First Field Guide: Birds* by Scott Weidensaul; and a blank journal, pen, and coloring pencils. The journal can be used for sketching and keeping track of the birds you see — their shapes, colors, and sizes, whether they chirp or sing, or any other interesting trait.

Backyard Bug Safari

You may think that only humans can garden, but the truth is, certain insects lend a hand in helping vegetables grow. Here are a few you and your child can try to spy.

Dragonfly: Also called a sewing needle or snake dragon, this long-bodied, four-winged insect has been around for about 300 million years and likes to eat pesky mosquitoes.

Ladybug: These ladies (or gents) are usually red with black spots, but can be yellow, orange, or black. They're great at polishing off aphids, which feed on roses and broccoli.

Praying mantis: A master of disguise, this critter can blend in with its environment and is adept at catching flies and moths.

Walk in a Spider's Shoes

354 To catch its dinner, a spider spins a sticky silk web for unsuspecting insects to land on. So why doesn't the spider itself get stuck? One theory is that it covers its feet with an oily liquid. To see how this works, have your child rub a bit of shortening on his fingertips. Place a long strip of tape (sticky side up) on a table. Use shorter pieces to tape down the ends. Now your child can easily walk his fingers the length of the strip.

Brain Boosters

Ant Farm

353 An ant farm gives you a chance to see how hard ants work to dig tunnels and get food. We like this design (adapted from one in *Do Bees Sneeze?* by James K. Wangberg), which is made with things from your recycling bin.

MATERIALS

2 widemouthed plastic jars that fit fairly
    closely one inside the other (we used
    1-quart and $\frac{1}{2}$-gallon jars)
Sandy soil
Sponge, bottle cap, corn syrup, and string
Scrap paper and black paper
Plastic wrap, rubber bands, and a pin

Place the smaller jar inside the larger one and fill the gap between the two with soil. Wet the sponge and place it in the smaller jar, along with a capful of corn syrup. Dangle several lengths of string from the soil in the larger jar to the bottom of the small jar so the ants can reach their food and water.

Now look around your neighborhood for ants (under parental supervision, as ants can bite). When you find an area with lots of ants, put down a sheet of paper with a bit of corn syrup on it. When several dozen ants have gathered on the paper, quickly transfer them to the jar. Cover the mouth of the jar with plastic wrap, secure it with a rubber band, and use a pin to poke airholes (smaller than the ants!) through the plastic. Wrap black paper around the jar (secure it with another rubber band) to keep the ant farm in the dark. When you remove the paper in a day or two, you should see the beginnings of a network of tunnels. Add more syrup and water, as needed. When you're done observing, release the ants where you found them.

A Sky Chart

355 This simple wheel is an ideal way for younger kids to keep track of the weather. Just divide a paper plate into sections that correspond to the weather conditions that are common to where you live and have your child color them in. Cut a pointer from another paper plate. With a paper fastener, loosely attach it to the center of the wheel and spin it to the section that reflects the day's weather.

WEATHER-WISE

Get Lost in the Clouds

356 Look up. What do you see in the clouds? Puffy dinosaurs? Flying mustaches? Meteorologists classify clouds by their shapes. For fun, see if you and your child can figure out which of the following categories the clouds you see fall into. Stratus clouds make a low, uniform sheet, like fog, and can produce only a drizzle. Nimbostratus are dark and wet-looking with, oftentimes, streaks of rain extending from them to the ground.

Cumulus are puffy and ever changing, and tend to resemble cauliflower. Also dubbed fair weather clouds, they usually form in the warm day air, then disappear at night. Cumulonimbus are the towering thunderheads whose tops are often flattened by upper-level winds. Cirrus, made of ice crystals, form high in the sky and look thin, wispy, and feathery. Cirrocumulus are thin clouds that form a wavy pattern, creating what's often referred to as a mackerel sky.

High cirrus clouds wander over...

Time Traveling

When we gaze at the stars, we are, in effect, looking back in time. That's because the light we see takes hundreds of years to reach us. On a clear night, invite your child to pretend she is a star sending light through time by pointing a flashlight toward the North Star. After a few seconds, explain that because the North Star is 780 light-years away, it would be the year 2780 before her "star" beam was visible there. In the meantime, the light would travel about 6 trillion miles per year!

JEFFMOORES.COM

CONSTELLATION CRAFT

Shining Stars

357 With this handy star-gazing device, your kids won't have to wait until nighttime to view their favorite constellations.

Instead, they can cast their own stellar images on a wall or ceiling in a darkened room.

MATERIALS

> Marker
>
> Large paper cup
>
> Pushpin or thumbtack
>
> Flashlight

Draw a constellation, such as Cassiopeia, the Northern Cross, or the Big or Little Dipper, on the bottom of a large paper cup. (For reference, you may want to pick up an astronomy book at your local library or science and nature store. Or you can search for an astronomy site on-line.) Then use the pushpin to make a small hole in the center of each star.

Now turn off the lights and hold the cup so that the bottom is pointing toward a wall. Shine the flashlight into the open end of the cup, angling it a bit to diffuse the rays, and enjoy the starry view.

CONSTELLATIONS

Eye Orion

For centuries, Orion the hunter has been the most luminous constellation in the winter sky. The seven supergiant stars that form his figure are much larger and thousands of times brighter than our sun. On a clear night, see if you can spot them (there are two at his shoulders, two at his knees, and three on his belt). Then look for the dimmer stars that outline his right arm (held above his head) and a shield in his left hand.

World Cultures

MIDDLE EAST CRAFT

Moroccan Castanets

358 The Berbers are a people with a long tradition of lively music and storytelling. Among their distinctive instruments are metal *qaraqib* — large castanets. This adaptation, made from a pair of 2-inch-diameter juice bottle lids, can be made and played in minutes. Here's how: first, create fingerholds by using strips of plastic tape to attach a wide rubber band to the top of each lid. Then use a 4-inch length of tape to hinge together the lids (with their insides facing) on one side. For a festive touch, tape a few strands of colorful curled ribbon to the hinge of the castanets, and you're ready to start tapping!

MAP READING

Get Global Perspective

359 Pump up your children's enthusiasm for geography with a globe. Besides gaining familiarity with the world's continents, countries, and cities, your kids will always be ready to pinpoint where something comes from. Next time you get mail postmarked from a distant locale, have them find the letter's origin. Or as you're putting away groceries, have them locate the home country of the olive oil or sardines. You can even spin the globe and plot out a pretend trip.

FAMILYFUN READER IDEA

Map Matters

Janae McSpadden of Amarillo, Texas, struggled with geography as a child and didn't want her daughter, Lacy, age ten, to have the same experience. So she gave it a place of honor in their home by keeping a laminated world map on their kitchen table. At dinnertime, the family talks about current events and locates where they are taking place. The map has also become an engaging conversation piece when they have dinner guests. "If there's ever a dead spot in a conversation, someone says, 'Oh, look, I've been there,' and we talk about places all over the world," Janae says. "It's been a wonderful family activity, and all it cost was $4.99."

What a Kick

360 Parts of Indonesia get up to 150 inches of rain in a year! No wonder Indonesian kids kick up their heels when the sun comes out — in an outdoor game called *main karet gelang* (rubber band game). To play, just wrap a bunch of rubber bands into a wad, as shown, then see how many times you can kick it into the air before it hits the ground. To learn about more games from other countries, pick up a copy of *Sidewalk Games Around the World*.

Celebrate an International Holiday

Come May Day, the Fennelly family of Upper Darby, Pennsylvania, gets up at dawn. Wearing bells around their ankles, the five kids run outside, stamp their feet, and hit the ground with sticks to wake the earth. And May Day is just one of the dozens of holidays the Fennellys celebrate each year to learn about other cultures. They shake maracas on Cinco de Mayo. For Oktoberfest, they eat hot dogs and listen to German oompah music. But the kids' favorite is Kattestoet, or Festival of the Cats, a holiday in Belgium. On that day, the children wear homemade cat masks and drink milk right out of bowls! Mom Robin keeps a notebook of the family's favorite international holidays so they can plan on celebrating them all again the next year.

Paper Girls

361 One holiday that Japanese girls look forward to with great excitement is Hina Matsuri (March 3rd), a day dedicated entirely to dolls. The tradition dates back hundreds of years and often features elaborate silk costumes. With these directions, your child can create her own collection of dolls dressed in origami kimonos.

MATERIALS

Poster board, red and black construction paper

Colored markers

Tape

From the poster board, cut out a simple doll's body that measures about 7 inches tall (it should resemble a large, round-headed clothespin). Trim below the head to create sloping shoulders.

For the kimono, cut out a 6-inch square from the red paper. From the black paper, cut out a 6- by ⅜-inch sash and a wig. In the center of the wig, cut a horizontal opening wide enough to accommodate the doll's head.

With colored markers, draw on a face. Next, form a collar by folding down

the top of the kimono ⅜ inch from the edge. Color it.

Lay the kimono flat so that the folded collar is facedown. Fit the wig onto the doll's head and then center the body on top of the kimono. Fold a top corner of the kimono down over the doll's shoulder.

Working on the same side of the kimono, fold the paper vertically to cover the doll's body. Use the same method to fold the opposite side of the kimono. Wrap the sash around the doll from front to back and tape together the ends.

A Food Odyssey

For too long, the three basic food groups for ten-year-old Patrick O'Brien of Oxnard, California, were a hamburger, fries, and a Coke. His mom, Susan, decided to broaden his gustatory horizons with a tour of restaurants specializing in international cuisines. In the process, Patrick has received a wholesome lesson in world cultures. "Our first outing was a Greek restaurant," remembers Susan. Not only did Patrick devour grape leaves and eggplant — nothing short of a miracle — but also mother and son talked about Greek culture, observed the staff, and listened to the restaurant's music. "Our waiter showed us maps and photos of where he was from," Susan says, "and told stories about his village." The O'Briens left with great memories and a takeout menu and place mat, now standard souvenirs of their monthly outings. "We've met some wonderful people, and Patrick is more willing to try new things in this format," says Susan. Next on the itinerary: India, Thailand, and the American South.

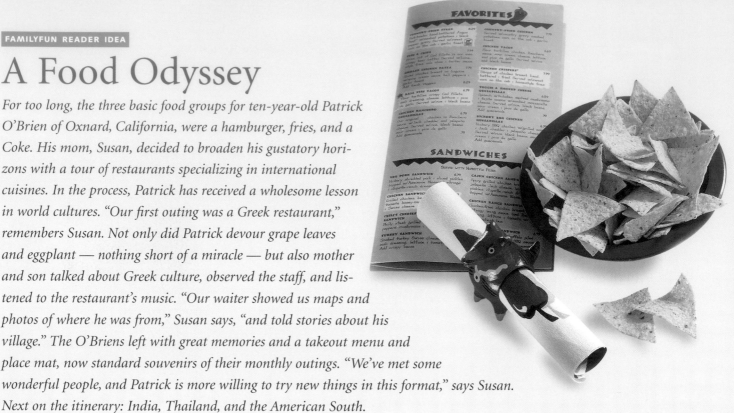

Around-the-world Dinners

362 For a real international learning experience, prepare a meal at home and get your kids in on the menu planning and cooking. You can even start the adventure with a family trip to your local library to check out an ethnic cookbook. After dinner, watch a video filmed in the country of choice.

Italian Night: Make pesto or shape pizza dough into single-serving pies so everyone can pile on the topping combination of his or her choice. Play an Italian opera to set the mood, and *mangia*!

Chinese Take-in: Try making steamed dumplings, sesame noodles, or moo shu pork. For atmosphere, string up colorful paper lanterns.

Mexican Fiesta: Chop tomatoes for spicy salsa, mix up some guacamole, and lay out a make-your-own taco or burrito buffet *grande*.

AFRICAN CRAFT

Adire Cloth

363 The Yoruba people of Nigeria use a dye-resist process called *adire* (*a-DEER-ay*) to adorn cloth with interesting symbols. Here's how your child can try his hand at the technique, using acrylic paint instead of messy ink, to create a decorative table runner.

MATERIALS

- Plain white muslin
- Masking tape
- Newspaper
- Stencils (optional)
- Paintbrushes
- Vegetable shortening
- Acrylic paints
- Water

Trim the muslin to a length and width that will serve as a good-size runner for your table, then tape the runner to several sheets of newspaper (to reduce the mess). Next, tape the whole project to a table or board (to keep the cloth taut).

Have your child lightly pencil a row of stencils or bold hand-drawn shapes onto the cloth. Using a paintbrush, apply a thick layer of vegetable shortening on each design. Explain that this process will keep the designs from absorbing color when you paint the cloth. Thin the acrylic paint with a little water so that it is the consistency of yogurt and paint the entire runner, even over the designs. Let the cloth dry completely (it may take overnight). Then peel it off the newspaper and rinse it in water with a little soap to remove the vegetable shortening and any bits of newspaper. Hang up your cloth to dry. If you want a finished edge, fold over a hem and secure it with fabric tape or glue.

EUROPEAN GAME

Swedish Sweep

364 Here's a quick game that kids in Sweden love to play. One child piles four marbles pyramid style in the middle of a 10-foot-wide chalk circle (this may take a few attempts, but it can be done). A second child tries to bombard the pyramid with a marble of his own and win whichever marbles roll out of the circle as a result. Then it's his turn to build a pyramid for the next person.

EGYPTIAN CRAFT

Sugar Cube Pyramid

365 It took 2,500,000 stones to build the Great Pyramid of Giza, where King Khufu was laid to rest with all of his earthly treasures. Using log sledges, workers rolled the massive blocks up mud ramps and slid them into place so precisely that a piece of paper can't fit between them. Here's how your kids can try their hand at Egyptian-style construction by turning a pile of sugar cubes into a model pyramid. Start by assembling the base. Using store-bought white frosting and a butter knife, "glue" together ten rows of ten sugar cubes each. Next, glue together the rows to form a square. For the second layer, glue together nine rows of nine cubes each, then center and glue the layer on top of the base square. Use this method to add seven more layers, each time decreasing the length of the rows by one cube. Finally, top the pyramid with a single cube.

Brain Boosters

Boredom Busters Index

Index

Art & Photography Credits

Special thanks to the following *FamilyFun* magazine photographers, illustrators, and stylists for their excellent work:

Photographers

A. Anderson/Pictor: *100 (top)*

Susan Barr: *82, 83 (top right and left)*

Robert Benson: *74 (top), 192*

Robert Bossi: *98 (bottom), 128, 129 (top), 130 (top, bottom), 131 (bottom)*

Katie Deits/Camera Graphics: *33 (license plates)*

Peter N. Fox: *Back cover (upper left & right), 8, 10 (bottom left), 13 (bottom left), 16, 21, 24 (left), 25, 30 (top, bottom left), 31 (top), 35, 44, 45, 46, 47 (bottom), 48 (bottom), 49 (top), 50 (top right), 52 (bottom), 53 (bottom), 59 (top), 60, 61 (middle), 62, 63, 66 (top right, bottom), 67 (top, middle), 87 (top right), 91 (bottom left), 99 (bottom right), 101 (bottom left), 102, 103, 106 (bottom), 107 (top, middle), 108 (top, bottom), 113, 116 (left), 118, 120, 121, 124 (bottom), 125 (top), 126 (top), 134, 138 (right), 141, 142 (bottom), 147, 150 (bottom), 156, 157 (top right, bottom), 158, 160 (bottom), 161, 162, 165, 195 (bottom right), 207*

Furnald/Gray: *114*

Andrew Greto: *13 (bottom right), 47 (top), 86, 143, 184 (bottom)*

Thomas Heinser: *Back cover (middle right), 42, 51 (bottom), 61 (bottom), 64 (bottom)*

Jacqueline Hopkins: *Back Cover (top middle), 166, 169 (middle)*

Tom Hopkins: *50 (bottom right), 66 (top left), 210 (right)*

Ed Judice: *Cover, Back Cover (bottom three), 9, 11 (top, bottom left & right), 12, 13 (top, bottom middle), 15 (bottom), 17, 18, 19, 20 (middle), 22 (top), 23, 24 (top & bottom right), 26, 27, 28, 29, 30 (bottom right), 31 (bottom), 32, 34, 36 (right), 37, 40 (top), 41 (left), 51 (top), 52 (top), 55 (top), 56 (bottom left), 68, 69, 71, 72, 73, 75, 76, 77, 78, 79, 80 (right), 81, 83 (bottom), 84, 87 (bottom), 88, 89, 90, 91 (top, middle, bottom right), 92 (top, middle), 94 (top), 95, 96, 97, 98 (top), 99 (top, bottom left), 101 (bottom right), 104 (right), 105 (right), 106 (top), 108 (middle), 110 (bottom), 111 (top), 112 (middle), 115 (bottom), 116 (right), 122, 123, 124 (top), 126 (bottom), 127 (top), 129 (bottom), 130 (middle), 131 (top), 132 (top), 135, 136, 137, 139, 140, 142 (top), 144, 145 (top), 148, 149, 150 (top, middle), 151, 152, 153, 154 (top), 155 (left), 157 (top left), 159, 163, 164, 169 (bottom), 170 (top), 171 (bottom), 174 (top, bottom right), 183 (left), 186 (top), 187 (top), 189 (top right, middle), 193, 194, 195 (top, bottom left), 196 (bottom), 197 (bottom), 198, 199 (top), 200, 201 (top left), 202, 203 (top, bottom), 204, 205, 206, 208 (top, bottom right), 209, 210 (left), 211, 212, 213, 214 (top), 215, 224*

Al Karevy: *117*

Brian Leatart: *101 (top)*

George D. Lepp/Natural Selection: *208 (bottom left)*

Lightworks Photographic: *39 (top), 170 (bottom)*

Marcy Maloy: *38, 39 (bottom), 40 (top), 85*

Robert Manella: *33 (bottom), 36 (left)*

David Martinez: *154 (bottom), 155 (right)*

Tom McWilliam: *53 (top), 65 (bottom), 87 (top left, middle), 182 (top), 183 (right), 214 (bottom)*

Peter Saloutos/The Stock Market: *57 (top)*

Joanne Schmaltz: *89, 93 (right), 104 (left), 109 (right), 132 (bottom left), 133 (top), 167, 172, 175 (bottom left), 178 (top), 186 (bottom), 190, 191 (bottom), 203 (middle)*

Shaffer/Smith Photography: *10 (top right), 11 (bottom middle), 14, 41 (top right), 43, 48 (top, middle), 56 (top), 55 (bottom), 65 (top), 67 (bottom), 94 (bottom), 100 (middle), 111 (bottom), 127 (bottom), 145 (bottom), 146 (top), 168, 169 (top), 171 (top, middle), 173, 175 (top middle, bottom right), 176, 177, 178 (bottom), 179, 180, 181, 182 (bottom), 184 (top), 185, 187 (bottom), 188, 189 (top left, bottom), 191 (top), 196 (top), 197 (top), 199 (bottom)*

Brian Smith: *54, 55 (bottom), 56 (bottom right), 57 (bottom), 58*

Steve Smith: *64 (top)*

Team Russell: *59 (middle), 70, 93 (left), 105 (left), 107 (bottom), 110 (top), 112 (top), 115 (top), 119, 132 (bottom right)*

Illustrators

Douglas Bantz: *20, 75, 106, 112, 126, 141, 162, 211 (bottom), 219*

Eldon Doty: *78, 209*

Janet Drew: *152*

Leo Espinosa: *207*

John Hart: *125, 133*

Stanford Kay: *41*

Bruce Macpherson: *201*

Jeff Moores: *22, 38, 58, 100 , 118, 198, 199, 211 (top)*

Debbie Palen: *26, 37, 89, 90*

Kevin Rechin: *109, 124*

Donna Ruff: *74*

Stylists

Fazia Ali, Bonnie Anderson/Team, Grace Arias, Bonnie Aunchman-Goudreau, Laurie Baer, Melissa Boudreau/Team, Catherine Callahan, Mary Cates, Pamela Courtleigh, Erica Ell/Team, Susan Fox, Ron Garnica, Harriet E. Granthen, Anastasia Hagerstrom/Koko Represents, Karin Lidbeck, Marie Piraino, Karen Quatsoe, Edwina Stevenson, Karen Uzell, Stacey Webb, Lynn Zimmerman

**Geodesic dome,
page 140**

Also from FamilyFun magazine

* **FamilyFun magazine:** a creative guide to all the great things families can do together. Call 800-289-4849 for a subscription.

* **FamilyFun Cookbook:** a collection of more than 250 irresistible recipes for you and your kids, from healthy snacks to birthday cakes to dinners everyone in the family can enjoy (Disney Editions, $24.95).

* **FamilyFun Crafts:** a step-by-step guide to more than 500 of the best crafts and activities to do with your kids (Disney Editions, $24.95).

* **FamilyFun Parties:** a complete party planner featuring 100 celebrations for birthdays, holidays, and every day (Disney Editions, $24.95).

* **FamilyFun Cookies for Christmas:** a batch of 50 recipes for creative holiday treats (Disney Editions, $9.95).

* **FamilyFun Tricks and Treats:** a collection of wickedly easy crafts, costumes, party plans, and recipes for Halloween (Disney Editions, $14.95).

* **FamilyFun.com:** visit us at www.familyfun.com and search our extensive archives for games, crafts, recipes, and other boredom-busting activities.